WHAT YOUR COLLEAGUES ARE SAYING . . .

Tapping the Writer Within is an essential guide to restoring joy and purpose in the writing classroom. I couldn't imagine a timelier resource: In this rapidly transforming literacy climate, as AI models churn out impeccably organized essays in a heartbeat, this book reminded me that the only reason children will need to write themselves is if they **want** to—if writing is an actively delightful, playful experience. Cultivating joy in the writing classroom is therefore not "icing on the cake" but the most foundational element of all. Fletcher offers tools, prompts, and systems that empower children to "feel in the marrow of their bones" that they are writers from the inside out and to always remember that they have beautiful, important ideas to contribute to our world. This deeply moving, often funny, practical book belongs in every classroom.

Lily Howard Scott, author of *The Words That Shape Us*

For the past thirty years, Ralph Fletcher has been helping me teach writing. In *Tapping the Writer Within: Practical Ways to Help All Students Claim Their Wri-dentity,* he gives writing teachers the inspiration and practical classroom advice they need. His focus on wri-dentity reminds us of the power of positioning students as writers, and he helps us see how to put writers at the center of the writing classroom. Through it all, Ralph's personal stories and classroom strategies feel like, once again, a friend and colleague is helping me teach writing.

Beth Rimer, Ohio Writing Project Director,
Miami University

As Ralph Fletcher always does, he has written a book for teachers that regrounds us and reminds us what is most important in the teaching of writing. By exploring writer identity as a key to supporting writers, he helps us see what is possible when we commit to seeing each and every child as a writer, so that they can begin to see themselves as writers.

Franki Sibberson, literacy consultant and author of
Classroom Design for Student Agency (NCTE, 2023) and
In Community with Readers (Stenhouse, 2024)

Tapping the Writer Within: Practical Ways to Help All Students Claim Their Wri-dentity by Ralph Fletcher validates my own identity and core beliefs as a writing teacher. He prioritizes knowing students, celebrating productive struggle, balancing support with challenge, and keeping authenticity at the center of their writing lives. With his unwavering commitment to all students seeing themselves as writers, Ralph shines a light on the importance of writing and provides powerful, practical ideas for building students' competence, confidence, and worth.

Melanie Meehan, founder of The Writing Clinic,
co-author of *Foundational Skills for Writing*,
and former curriculum specialist

Ralph Fletcher's work has shaped the way I think about writing, and this book will do so again. His insights into helping students discover their wri-dentity remind me why I love teaching writing. This is a must-read for teachers who want to help students see themselves as lifelong writers.

Sara Pommarane, Distinguished Teacher in Residence,
University of Wyoming

Cut through curriculum clutter with Ralph Fletcher's simple, joyful practices for building classrooms where children become writers for life. Ralph blends his stories, sample drafts, and trusted expertise with a chorus of wise educator and student voices telling us what kids need to be skilled, confident, and especially, happy to write.

Katherine Bomer, literacy consultant and author of
*The Journey Is Everything: Teaching Essays
That Students Want to Write for People
Who Want to Read Them* (Heinemann)

Ralph Fletcher, one of the most trusted voices in the teaching of writing, centers the essential role of developing an identity as a writer. *Tapping the Writer Within* is a thoughtful, specific, and practical guide for helping students develop their wri-dentity and igniting a lifelong passion for writing.

Lester Laminack, author and consultant

Tapping the
Writer Within

Tapping the Writer Within

Practical Ways to Help All Students
Claim Their Wri-dentity

Ralph Fletcher

CORWIN

FOR INFORMATION:

Corwin

A Sage Company

2455 Teller Road

Thousand Oaks, California 91320

(800) 233-9936

www.corwin.com

Sage Publications Ltd.

1 Oliver's Yard

55 City Road

London EC1Y 1SP

United Kingdom

Sage Publications India Pvt. Ltd.

10th Floor, Emaar Capital Tower 2

MG Road, Sikanderpur

Sector 26, Gurugram

Haryana - 122002

India

Sage Publications Asia-Pacific Pte. Ltd.

18 Cross Street #10-10/11/12

China Square Central

Singapore 048423

Vice President and
  Editorial Director: Monica Eckman

Executive Content Leader: Elizabeth Gildea

Content Development Editor: Melissa Rostek

Associate Content Development &
  Operations Manager: Zachary Vann

Product Assistant: Vanessa Brown

Production Editor: Neelu Sahu

Copy Editor: Diana Breti

Typesetter: C&M Digitals (P) Ltd.

Proofreader: Lawrence Baker

Cover Designer: Gail Buschman

Library of Congress Control Number: 2025048084

Paperback ISBN: 978-1-0719-9863-2

Contents

Foreword

As a writing consultant, I spend a lot of time in early childhood class-rooms, and I often launch book making right at the beginning of the year. On these days, it always strikes me how easy it seems for young children to build a writing identity. All it takes is to give children prestapled books and markers and let them have at it. Children move quickly from "I can't write" to "I guess I *can* write" to "I'm a writer." But even though it looks easy for children to build a writing identity, it's actually the result of the very specific decisions teachers make. Teachers who create writers

- believe children can write, even before they believe it themselves.

- honor their approximations of words and illustrations and are comfortable with them doing it the best they can.

- allow them to have ownership of what to write.

- show them how writing is fun, joyful, and playful.

- see beyond what's on the page and respond with wonderment and awe to children's incredible thinking.

- understand that writing includes composition, not only phonics and spelling.

- make writing easy and achievable.

It also strikes me that there are similar factors that impact adults' writing identities. For example, I'm not a very confident writer, something that surprised Ralph when we started talking about some of the ideas in this book. (Amazingly, he still asked me to write this foreword).

But while I'm not very confident, I do have a writing identity. I write frequently, on a regular basis, and I see myself as a writer.

So how did I develop this identity despite doubting my skill as a writer? I can point to similar factors that impact four and five year olds. I was fortunate to have editors like Kate Montgomery and Zoe Ryder White and a friend like Katie Wood Ray who nurtured me as a writer, in much the same way teachers support their students. These mentors

- saw me as a writer, even before I did.

- nurtured my emerging identity by noticing my strengths as a writer.

- built my strengths with small nudges forward, careful to not overwhelm and hinder my emerging identity.

- supported me in becoming a better writer incrementally, bit by bit over time.

- honored my approximations of writing.

- valued my ideas and composition, beyond my ability to write in a conventionally correct way.

And I had mentors in the form of professional books and authors who provided a pathway for me to envision what I wanted to do. I had mentors like Ralph Fletcher, whose books supported me as a teacher and principal, but even more so as an author.

Ralph realizes that the factors that impact writing identity—or, as Ralph calls it, *wri-dentity*—hold true for anyone, adult or child. He knows how important it is for children to develop strong writing identities. Identities that make children eager to write about personally important topics. Identities that make children eager to share their writing. Identities reinforced by engagement that makes them more skillful and improves the quality of their writing.

Ralph also knows how easy it is for children to lose their writing identity. The big and small decisions teachers make over time either support or diminish children's identities. That's what makes this book so important.

Wri-dentity is especially important given the educational environment today, in which more and more students encounter writing programs that needlessly crush their writing identities. Programs that never let students choose their topic or genre. Programs that don't allow students to write authentic pieces, in which their teacher is their only audience. Programs that rely on misguided, one-size-fits-all instruction that assumes all students need the same thing, same day, same time.

Ralph shows us how to counter this unfortunate trend. Throughout *Tapping the Writer Within,* Ralph shows us how to nurture children's identities, in big and small ways, regardless of the structure of the writing program or approach to writing. Every teacher will find ideas they can use in their class right away.

Further, Ralph implores us to back up our beliefs about identity with actions. As Ralph says in Chapter 6, "Sometimes you need to take a stand. Sometimes you have to close your door and do what you know is right." We have to take Ralph's advice. He's not saying to ignore curriculum and standards or jeopardize your job, but he is saying that we have to balance what we might be required to do with what we know about how children learn.

To help us do this, throughout the book, Ralph shares specific examples from teachers who are doing this work every day. Ralph has interviewed teachers from a wide variety of contexts who all value the importance of supporting children's identities. It provides us with a sense of a community of teachers who are in this together. If they can do it, we can too.

Ralph brings his extensive expertise and a unique perspective to thinking about identity. He writes from his experience as a writing consultant and author of professional development books and as the author of picture books, poetry, and novels for children. The immense volume of beautiful writing Ralph has created allows him to share ideas that he has used with children and that have also impacted him.

Ralph shows us the role of published mentor texts in supporting writing identities, and he also emphasizes the importance of writing ourselves. It's difficult to support writing identities if we don't have that identity ourselves. Ralph also shares his own formative, playful writing that demonstrates how easy this can be. Importantly, he gives us permission to be comfortable with our own approximations as writers. Ralph says, "Think of yourself as an *imperfect mentor* for the young writers in your class. It may seem counterintuitive but it's true: it's your imperfection that make it possible for them to learn from you" (Chapter 9).

Ralph shares too many powerful strategies to name here, but I do need to call out one more. The title of Chapter 13 says it all: Let Them Mess Around and Play. Writing can be messy, something children don't always see or understand. They see beautiful, funny, clever writing and think it just came out that way. They don't realize how much authors tinker and revise and, well, . . . play. Ralph advocates for an immediate release of control, so that children are so eager to write they jump in and give it a try.

In their essay in *The Teacher You Want to Be*, Peter Johnston and Gay Ivey start by noting that, "When lists of 'standards' for schools are made, nobody seems concerned that happiness is not on the list" (Glover & Keene, 2015, p. 51). They make the case that student well-being has an impact on learning. What would happen if there was a standard that said, "Children will enjoy reading"? If it was valued and measured, it would certainly impact what occurs in classrooms.

Ralph makes the same case for writing identity. How would schools change if we valued and measured writing identity? What would happen to students and their writing if we prioritized identity, engagement, and confidence? What if we used identity as the foundation for supporting more skilled, accomplished writers? Fortunately, Ralph isn't waiting for standards to change. By following Ralph's wise lead, we can impact the children we work with, as well as start conversations that impact broader, schoolwide change. We can help our students see themselves as—and truly become—writers.

If we value children's writing identity, then we must support it. As teachers we need support as well; *Tapping the Writer Within* is exactly what we need.

Matt Glover
Author and Literacy Consultant

Acknowledgments

"Jordan Peele has a new movie," a friend says. Impressive! But when you see the film, and watch the credits, you realize that hundreds of other people were involved in creating it. The Jordan Peeles and Greta Gerwigs of the world, however talented they might be, can't do it alone. And the same principle holds true here. I may be the author of this book, but many other people contributed their time, efforts, and wisdom. Without their help, this book wouldn't exist, period.

I conversed with many educators: Katherine Bomer, Colleen Cruz, Donna Santman, Lynne Dorfman, Angela Faulhaber, Georgia Heard, Martha Horn, Peter Johnston, Ellin Keene, Barry Lane, Melanie Meehan, Tom Newkirk, Katie Wood Ray, Stacey Shubitz, Jeff Wilhelm, and Alan J. Wright. Thank you, guys! I respect you so much. Our back-and-forth dialogues helped me shape and reshape my thinking.

Major thanks go to Carl Anderson, Kelly Gallagher, Matt Glover, Penny Kittle, Tasha Laman, and Sharon Zumbrunn. You were extremely generous with your time and wisdom. No surprise that your fingerprints are all over this book.

Thanks to Gina Dignon for giving the book a thoughtful read before it went to final revisions.

I interviewed many teachers whose perspectives helped keep my thinking practical and classroom-based. Thanks to Grant Bearden, Ana Chavez, Tracy Cole, Amy Crehore, Ellen Ervin, Mike Reynolds, Lisa Rose, and Katie Tingle.

I'm especially grateful to Sara Tillett, Amy Horton, and Emily Callahan, who not only shared their wisdom but also did the tedious work of chasing down permissions for their students' work. Thanks, guys!

Thanks to Michelle Rue, Olivia Wahl, and Destiny Diaz.

Thanks to Dan Feigelson and Mike McCormick, insightful educators and two of my closest friends.

Thanks to Nikki Grimes and Nawal Qarooni for sharing your journeys in coming to see yourselves as writers.

For the past few summers, Georgia Heard and I led the Quoddy Writing Retreat in Downeast Maine. Each retreat gave me the opportunity to work closely with twenty-five writers. It was illuminating to participate in their journey, to watch them gradually come to see themselves as writers. I'm grateful to each one of them.

In writing this book, I drew upon experiences from my family, watching as my kids developed their writing selves. Thanks to Taylor Curtis, Adam Curtis, Robert Fletcher, and Joseph Fletcher.

My own wri-dentity has been nurtured by working with a number of wonderful editors: Christy Ottaviano, Holly Price, Liz Gildea, and Nina Ignatowicz.

I'm thankful for the students who allowed me to include their writing and drawings in this book. Your candid perspectives are crucial elements of this book. Many thanks to Aaron, Solomon, Max, Kalina, Bennett, Vivi, Ellis, Emi, Emersyn, and Ruby. Thanks also to Elliot Nichols, Emma Templeton, Henry Wahl, Natalia Szubielski, Reese Basquet, and Jorja Derosier.

Thanks to JoAnn, my bee-wife and real wife. I'm grateful to you for your unwavering support, for making it fun and keeping it real.

Publisher's Acknowledgments

Corwin gratefully acknowledges the following reviewers for their contributions.

Carl Anderson
Author and Literacy Consultant
Brooklyn, NY

Katherine Bomer
Author and National Writing Consultant
Denton, TX

Jacie Maslyk
Instructional Coach
Coraopolis, PA

Sara Pommarane
Distinguished Teacher in Residence, The University of Wyoming
Laramie, WY

About the Author

Ralph Fletcher's books for young readers include *Fig Pudding, Flying Solo, Marshfield Dreams: When I Was a Kid,* and *The Writer's Notebook: Unlocking the Writer Within.* Ralph has published many books for writing teachers including *Joy Write: Cultivating High-Impact Low-Stakes Writing, What a Writer Needs, Writing Workshop: The Essential Guide,* and *Focus Lessons: How Photography Enhances the Teaching of Writing.* Ralph believes in student choice, authentic voice, and writing as a form of self-discovery. He frequently visits schools and speaks at educational conferences around the world, helping teachers find wiser ways of teaching writing. www.ralphfletcherbooks.com

Introduction

I was coaching a fourth-grade soccer team. It was the last game of the season, and we really needed the win. We were down 5–4 with about ten minutes left in the game. I made eye contact with our three best players—Justin, Rachel, and Devon—sitting on the bench. I knew that they knew that I knew they would be absolutely crucial if we were to pull this game out.

I put them into the game. Two minutes later, Rachel streaked down the right side and tied the score.

We had another player, Abby, sitting on the bench. She had limited skills and, as a result, lacked confidence. Abby was most comfortable playing defense where her limitations wouldn't stick out. But when Devon turned an ankle I needed a healthy player, so I sent Abby in to substitute for him. She gave me a dubious look.

"Really? You want me to play forward?"

"You can do it," I told her. "Be aggressive."

A few minutes later we had the ball near the opposing team's goal. Suddenly the ball squirted out and rolled in front of Abby.

"Shoot!" I yelled. "Shoot!"

Abby raced in and took the shot. The ball hit the near post and bounced aside. We lost the game 6–5. Afterward Abby came over to me. She looked dazed.

"I almost scored," she murmured. "Did you see that? I almost scored!"

"You came that close!" I agreed.

As she looked up, I saw her expression change.

"That was really cool," she told me. "You know, I should have played on offense more. I wish I had."

I still think about Abby. She wasn't a strong player. She didn't see herself as a soccer player and, to be honest, neither did I. She seemed like a kid who was content to wear the uniform and otherwise stay in the background. But look what nearly happened when she got the chance to play offense! I realize now that I sold that kid short. I should have believed in her. She might have resisted, but I should have pushed her, at least a little, to discover what she had to offer.

A few years later, I visited a fifth-grade classroom in the Bronx, New York. I had never met the teacher before. She greeted me when I walked in and touched three students on their shoulders.

"These are my writers—one, two, three," she said. "The rest of them are strictly average. Not a superstar in the group."

Ouch. That moment will haunt me forever. It must have been empowering for the three kids whose shoulders she touched, the ones she endowed with heightened status by declaring them writers. How nice is that! But what about the other kids? How must they have felt? What was their pathway to claiming that identity?

Seeing yourself as a soccer player shouldn't be reserved for the very best players on the team. And being declared a writer shouldn't be a special gift bestowed on a lucky few, either. I say spread the wealth. I'm channeling Oprah Winfrey: Everybody gets a juicer! Everybody's a writer!

Unfortunately, we're miles away from that. I feel for kids in today's writing classrooms. Even in elementary school where students are having their first encounters with writing, the writing I see is mostly academic: essays, compare-and-contrast, argument speech. What about real-life genres that most kids actually like to read? What about fairy tales and fantasy? How about fiction and poetry? Those players, the writers who might love those genres, have to sit on the bench. They'll be lucky if they ever get into the game.

The writing kids produce in school has very little connection to the writing we see, read, and value in the world at large. According to the National

Council of Teachers of English (NCTE) Position Statement on Writing Instruction in School (2022), "The ubiquity of standardized assessments, including high-stakes standardized assessments, perpetuate a limited view of composition. . . . Writing instruction often mirrors test preparation, with students filling in templates and following formulas rather than making important and intentional decisions about writing for authentic audiences and purposes."

How can children find their stride as writers if almost all they do is academic writing? An unrelenting diet of academic writing works against the goal of this book, which is to ignite passion in our students so they see themselves as writers.

I feel for writing teachers, too. Many teachers acknowledge that they don't feel confident about teaching writing. Most never took a preservice course on how to teach writing. In many districts, teachers are given a program and instructed to use it with fidelity. In other words, follow the script. There's little wiggle room, little chance to personalize it, to make it their own. At the same time, writing teachers must somehow juggle and satisfy a bewildering number of standards, competencies, benchmarks, district goals, and so on.

In his iconic trilogy *Lord of the Rings*, JRR Tolkien conceived of "one ring to rule them all." That got me thinking. What if there was one overarching goal in the writing classroom? One goal to rule them all, one goal to contain all the others?

Wri-Dentity

What It Is and Why It Matters

> Nurturing the writing identity of students must remain at the forefront of teachers' words and actions every time we enter the classroom.
>
> —Alan J. Wright, literacy coach

My grandson Solomon, age five, wanted me to read to him.

"Can we read that book about when you were growing up?" he asked.

"You mean *Marshfield Dreams*?"

"The one with the kid who always has to sleep under the kitchen table," he said.

"Oh, you mean *Fig Pudding*! Sure, but that's a chapter book."

"That's fine. Mom and Dad read lots of chapter books to me."

So we climbed on top of the bed, and I started reading *Fig Pudding*. Solomon giggled, enjoying the antics of the Abernathys, a family loosely based on my birth family. Afterward, Solomon stayed upstairs to read on his own while I went down to have lunch. I was eating a sandwich with his mother, Jess, when he came down to join us at the table.

"When Grandpa dies," Solomon announced, "I'm going to write a book about my childhood."

I half-choked on my grilled cheese sandwich.

"Wait—what?"

Jess chuckled and looked at Solomon. "You don't have to wait til Grandpa dies. You can write it right now!"

"Really?"

"Sure!"

So Solomon sat down to write. (See Photo 1.1.)

Photo 1.1
Solomon writing the story of his childhood.

At one point, Solomon wanted to write the word *show* but wasn't sure how to make the *sh* sound.

"When you put S and H together it makes the *shhhh* sound," I told him. (Note that he reversed the letters when he wrote them in his story.)

Solomon and I had a couple of impromptu writing conferences while he worked on his book. He had noticed that *Fig Pudding* was broken into chapters, each with its own title.

"When I'm done," he told me, "I'm going to go back and make a title for each chapter."

"Interesting. What title do you think you'll use for the first chapter?"

He thought for a moment before declaring, "Beetlejuice!"

That made me smile. Beetlejuice is a wonderful word, for sure, even if it seemed totally random. It struck me that Solomon didn't yet grasp the idea that the title of a particular chapter should be aligned with the contents of that chapter.

Solomon worked on his book for nearly an hour and borrowed a few text features from *Fig Pudding*. He noticed that in my book I had used a series of three asterisks as section breaks, and he did the same thing in his book. Later, Jess shared her perspective on her son's writing experience.

"I think Solomon was really struck by the fact that you had turned stories from when you were a kid—the kind of stories our family tells each other out loud when we're just hanging out together—into a real book," Jess said. "He already knew you were an author, but I think that reading *Fig Pudding* with you and knowing that he'd met some of the people in the stories made the possibility of being an author seem real and present. It's not just something that grownups can do because he already can tell the same kind of stories as you did in your book."

Later that day Solomon proudly read his book to me. When he finished, he beamed a big smile.

"I can be an author even when I'm just a kid."

Solomon was playing with a powerful idea: his identity as a writer. He hadn't claimed it yet, not quite, but he was trying it on for size.

On Writing Identity

In this book, I have combined the words *writing* and *identity* to create a new term: *wri-dentity*. It means *seeing oneself as a writer*.

In recent years, *identity* has become a charged word, one often used with extreme care and even caution: *How does he identify?* Or, *What was the role of identity politics in the election?*

> In this book, I have combined the words *writing* and *identity* to create a new term: *wri-dentity*. It means *seeing oneself as a writer*.

This book doesn't deal with identity in the cultural, social, or political sense of the word. Rather, I intend to explore identity in the most practical sense. In this book, *identity* refers to our sense of who we are as individuals and as members of a group. *I'm a surfer. I'm a knitter. I'm a brother.*

At its core identity is about belonging, and humans take great pleasure in joining one group or another. If you happen to be in Boston and stroll around the TD Garden arena before a Celtics game, you'll get swallowed by a sea of green. Everybody is wearing Celtics merchandise: hats, sweatshirts, jackets. I saw one guy wearing a T-shirt that proudly proclaimed I BLEED GREEN. Those fans are part of a club, eager to celebrate that sense of belonging and to connect with others who feel the same way.

Wearing swag for a favorite sports team or beloved rock star is one way to express your identity, but those external indicators only take you so far. Consider the world of photography. You can buy Sony's top-of-the-line camera with all the accessories—a telephoto lens, gimbal head, tripod, flash unit, plus a ThinkTank backpack to carry it all. All that gear may impress your friends, but it doesn't make you a photographer.

The same holds true for writing. A teacher could purchase an I AM AN AUTHOR! T-shirt for every student in class. That might create wonderful group photo, but thirty kids all wearing I AM AN AUTHOR! T-shirt doesn't make them authors or writers.

> Turns out there's no shortcut for creating wri-dentity.
>
> Turns out wri-dentity must be developed from the inside out.
>
> Before I prove to you that I'm a writer, I must prove it to myself.

Carl Anderson, author of *How to Become a Better Writing Teacher* (Anderson & Glover, 2023) and *Teaching Fantasy Writing* (Anderson, 2024), learned this lesson the hard way when he tried to impose writing identity on his eighth-grade students.

"At the beginning of the year I told every one of my classes that they would all be writers," Carl says ruefully. "Throughout the year, kids continued to poke fun at my declaration. One boy drew a caricature of me pointing at the class, saying, 'You are all writers.' My favorite student, Jasmine, wrote a poem that describes a lovely daydream she was having, one that shatters when I suddenly appear saying, 'You will all be writers in my class.' Those eighth graders made it clear that their identities were up to them and weren't going to be shaped by decree by their well-intentioned but misguided teacher!"

This may seem obvious—of course we want our students to see themselves as readers and writers. But schools haven't done a great job of helping students see themselves as writers. Several studies have shown that students don't enjoy writing (National Literacy Trust, 2024). And the aversion to writing doesn't end when they graduate. Kids bring their negative feelings about writing into adulthood. If you tell a group of adults, "Raise your hand if you are a reader," most hands will go up. But if you tell the same group of adults, "Now raise your hand if you are a writer," only a few people will raise their hands. Most people don't identify as writers, even though we use writing in many different ways.

Some literacy experts argue that the way writing is taught in school prevents kids from identifying as a writer.

"In too many classrooms children simply do not get the opportunity to write," says Tasha Laman, author of *From Ideas to Words* (2013). "And when they do write, they are prescribed a topic or prompt. There are still too many 'one and done' writing activities. These kinds of controlled writing situations send a clear identity message to students: *Writing is hard; you don't have anything worthy to write, so I will tell you what to write.*"

Wri-dentity is powerful, even transformational, but it is also fragile. Getting vaccinated for diphtheria when you're young will protect you from the disease for the rest of your life. But wri-dentity doesn't work that way. Students can see themselves as writers one year, but that wri-dentity can disappear the next.

In mid-October, I visited a school in Queens, New York, where I had worked as a writing consultant the previous year, doing demonstration teaching in writing instruction. A student called out to me:

"Mr. Fletcher! Mr. Fletcher!"

I stopped to peer at him. His figure made a silhouette against the bright light from the far window, and it took me a few moments to clearly see him: a slender boy with curly hair. I searched my memory but still couldn't place him. The boy took a few steps toward me.

"Carlos, from last year," he said, giving me a searching look. "Don't you remember? I was an author last year."

Why Wri-dentity Matters

Wri-dentity is an inside-out belief in yourself: *I'm a writer*. And it's not just a pretty notion—wri-dentity grounds students, gives them a firm foundation, creates a durable context for learning. Students who identify as writers are kids who have written a lot. They have created texts for a variety of purposes. These writing experiences help them build the flexible thinking that will be essential when faced with new writing challenges.

Writing great Don Murray said, "I don't teach students to write. I teach them how to reread their drafts." Kids with robust wri-dentity know their strengths (*I'm good at coming up with exciting plots*) as well as what they struggle with (*My stories can get confusing*). This helps them to be thoughtful and strategic as they reread their work and decide whether and how to revise it.

Kids with abundant wri-dentity aren't naïve. They understand that writing isn't easy. Sometimes it's a royal pain in the butt. Frustration and failure are part of the deal. Those kids know from experience that there will be good days and bad days when they write, but they have the grit and persistence to persevere when the writing is difficult.

Building Wri-dentity in the Classroom

This book is based on the philosophy of constructivism—Piaget's seminal idea that knowledge is socially constructed through experience. First and foremost, students will claim their wri-dentity by writing and by living in a community of writers.

"I can say I have an identity of myself as a marathon runner," says Matt Glover, author of *How to Become a Better Writing Teacher* (Anderson & Glover, 2023). "But to actually have that identity I have to get out and run some marathons. In order for students to have an identity as a writer, they need to write a lot."

This doesn't happen automatically. A writing teacher can play a pivotal role. And although teachers can't guarantee that every student will see themselves as writers, we can provide conditions that will make it more likely for this to happen.

"Children's writing identities will either thrive or fail to bloom according to what happens with the writing experiences encountered in the classroom," says Alan J. Wright, Australian-based literacy consultant and writer.

In this book, we'll look a practical steps teachers can take to build wri-dentity in the classroom. We're going to get granular and specific about exactly how to do that, but before we do, I'd like to put forth a few broad principles of wri-dentity:

- **Abundance.** The belief that *I am a writer* shouldn't be limited to a chosen few. Every student must be included.

- **Quantity.** Finding your stride as a writer involves a great deal of writing. Every writing teacher wants to see quality writing, but it turns out that quantity—volume—is a prerequisite.

- **Pleasure.** Kids will develop their wri-dentity if they experience the pleasure of writing. It's got to be fun, at least some of the time.

- **Diversity.** We tap the strength of any community when we tap its diversity. Each writer in your classroom is different; consequently, we must embrace the notion that every student's wri-dentity will be unique. And we have to roll out the red carpet for the "funds of knowledge" that every child brings into the classroom.

A student's wri-dentity is not some obscure trait but an integral part of their overall identity (i.e., their sense of who they are, how they think, how they learn, their place in the world). In their book *Writing for Pleasure*, Ross Young and Felicity Ferguson (2021b) put it like this: "Through writing and being a writer, children say, 'Hey world, here I am. This is me. This is what I think, feel, know, imagine and want to share with you'" (p. 163).

Claiming wri-dentity involves a transformation that's internal, not external. It happens when students feel it in the marrow of their bones: *I'm a writer.*

Establish Regular Routines

2

> I always get up and make a cup of coffee while it is still dark—it must be dark—and then I drink the coffee and watch the light come . . . And I realize that for me this ritual comprises my preparation to enter a space that I can only call non-secular.
>
> —Toni Morrison

Most writers follow a routine that is highly particular. And if that routine gets interrupted—whoa!—the gears come to a screeching halt. Don Murray was happy to share his writing routine:

Write early.

Write fast to outrun the censor in your head.

Count words.

Know your task before you sit down.

Write when you're not writing.

"I write for two hours in the morning," he once told me. "But it's what I do the other twenty-two hours that allows me to do that writing."

Nikki Grimes, author of the memoir *Ordinary Hazards*, had this to say about the way she writes:

"*Mise en place,* a French term, is the phrase that comes to mind," she told me. "Just as a chef prepares and organizes ingredients and equipment before cooking, the first thing I do is set out pads, pens, Post-its, whatever reference tools I might need, editorial notes (if any), character sketches, and character backstories. Once that's done, I'm ready to write without interruption."

I bring a cup of coffee into my office and write from 8:30 until 10, take a short break, and continue working until noon. I've found I'm freshest in the morning. Those hours provide my best shot at writing something half-decent. Professionals need consistent time to write, and apprentice writers need nothing less. It's essential to establish regular writing routines for your classroom.

Time

Writing in schools is too often sporadic and scarce. "Writing instruction in many English language arts classrooms rarely includes opportunities for children and youth to write often" (NCTE, 2022). If we want students to see themselves as writers, they need time to write that is ample, sustained, and daily.

Ample. Students need enough time so they can sink into the writing during each session.

Sustained. It will be difficult for kids to develop their wri-dentity if they only get fragments of time scattered here and there throughout the school day. They need a block of time to write.

Daily. In some classrooms, kids get to write on Monday but don't get another writing time until the following Monday. By then most of them have forgotten what they've written. With a schedule like that, how can they possibly find continuity, momentum, or flow? Kids need to be writing on a daily basis.

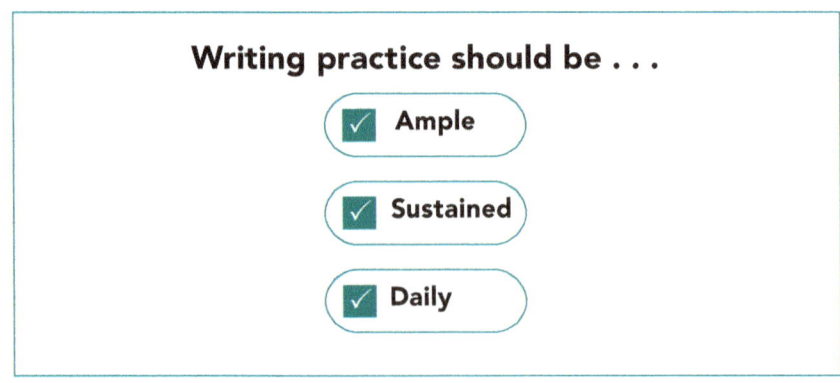

Once, when my son Joseph was four, he asked me to help him build something. I had just come into the house so I still had my coat on. I started to help Joseph, but he didn't seem happy.

"What's wrong?" I asked.

"Take your coat off, Daddy! When you've still got your coat on, I feel like you're gonna leave any minute!"

It shouldn't feel like we "have our coats on" when it's writing time in the classroom. In other words, it can't be a tentative time slot that gets usurped every time something more important comes along. It should be *dedicated time* deliberately set aside for students to sink into their writing.

What If I Don't Have Thirty Minutes to Devote to Writing?

You may be thinking, "All fine and good, but I'm required to follow the literacy program our district just purchased. I honestly don't have time in my daily schedule for my students to do thirty minutes of sustained writing. Is there anything I can do?"

Yes. You can still find small ways to infuse the principles of wri-dentity into your classroom. Here are a few tips and suggestions to get started:

- **Quick writes.** A five-minute quick write fits perfectly into odd times of the day, just after students arrive in the morning, or immediately after lunch recess.

- **Juicy prompts.** You might ask students, "Outside of school, what is one area where you're a straight A student? What makes you a straight A student?"

- **The daily morning message.** I talked with a few teachers who let their students create the daily morning message that gets written on the whiteboard. The teachers I talked to were struck by the way students put their own spin on, and brought their own voice (accompanied by humorous drawings) to, the messages they created.

(Continued)

(Continued)

- **High-interest genre.** See if you can substitute humor, fantasy, poetry, comics, sports writing, or another popular genre for one academic writing genre.

- **Share your writing with the class.** (See Chapter 5.) Make sure they know that writing is a part of your life.

- **Writer's notebook.** Show students your writer's notebook, and encourage them to keep their own idea book, stealth notebook, or writer's notebook. Find a few minutes for each kid to share one or two sentences from their notebook.

- **Greenbelt writing.** Let students know that you value "greenbelt writing" (see Chapter 13), in which they have total control over the writing they create.

- **Find some way to make writing fun.** I know one teacher who led students through a brief writing exercise. Then she ceremoniously brought the waste paper basket to the center of the room.

"Crumple up your paper," she told them. "Let's see who can throw it into the basket the first time you try."

After a moment of stunned silence, her students eagerly followed her instructions.

"I wanted to let those kids know that writing doesn't always have to be saved," she explained. "Writing is a way to develop your ideas. You can throw away your paper, but the thinking remains in your head."

It's interesting that we talk about time as a commodity we spend, like money. The amount of time we spend on a particular task or interest reveals how much (or how little) we value it.

Devoting time to an activity is a way to claim identity. In his book *Outliers*, Malcolm Gladwell (2008) popularized the idea that a person must spend about 10,000 hours to get proficient in a complex skill. We can debate the precise number, but there's no doubt that spending time doing something is essential if you want to get good at it. If I spend ninety minutes playing guitar each morning, I might eventually see myself as a guitar player. Our students need to write on a daily basis in order to see themselves as writers.

Establishing Space and Structure in the Writing Classroom

When we talk about goal setting we usually focus on student goals, but I have my own goals in the writing classroom. I divide them into short-term goals and long-term goals. At the beginning of the year, I focus on three short-term goals:

1. Establish structure and routines for the writing workshop.

2. Create a safe environment.

3. Help kids love writing time.

This is a short list, and you could make it even shorter by combining numbers two and three. It's been my experience that kids will love to write if they feel they're in a safe environment.

Think about your physical classroom. What spaces do you need? How will your students use them? You may decide you need a

- **meeting space** where the whole class can convene for mini-lessons, read-alouds, and share time;

- **author's chair** specially designated for students to share writing with the class;

- **writing center** where students can easily access resources they need, such as writing folders, extra paper, stapler, markers, thesaurus, etc.;

- **classroom library** where you can store and display student writing.

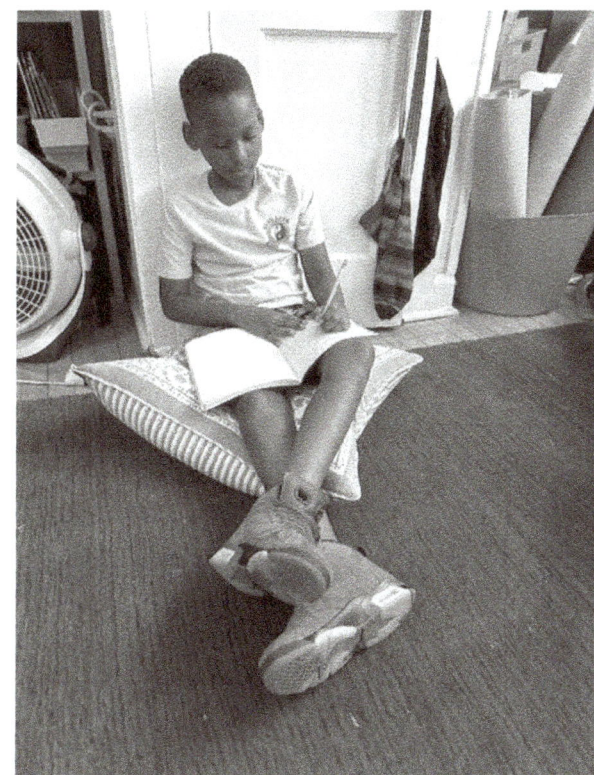

Photo 2.1
Students may feel more comfortable writing on the floor or at a station away from their desk.

In their book *Welcome to Writing Workshop*, Stacey Shubitz and Lynne Dorfman (2019) put it like this: "Students need to be able to move around the room to gather resources, find places to write comfortably, discuss their writing with others, and receive immediate feedback" (p. 44).

How will you structure the writing time? I recommend the structure used in many writing workshop classrooms: mini-lesson, writing time, share. I endorse numerous features of the writing workshop: the short, targeted mini-lessons; the emphasis on student writing; the invaluable one-to-one teacher/student writing conference; and the share session at the end. If there's a better approach to teaching writing, well, I haven't found it.

However, some teachers opt to structure their classroom in other ways. One teacher I know starts by having his students open their notebooks and engage in a five-minute quick write. He says, "My feeling is, BOOM: let's get those writing muscles moving!" After that, he gathers the kids for an ultra-quick share session. Then he does a mini-lesson and sends the kids off to write.

Whatever structure you decide for your writing classroom, it should be "reassuringly consistent" (Young & Ferguson, 2021b). This is a paradox that has always intrigued me: The most creative work is usually done in the most predictable structure. This axiom holds true for young writers; they need to know what to expect.

> Whatever structure you decide for your writing classroom, it should be "reassuringly consistent."—Ross Young and Felicity Ferguson

I care a great deal about craft in writing. However, my first goal is to establish the routines, rituals, and structure of the writing classroom. If everybody knows what to do during writing time, things will run more smoothly. But it's more than simply avoiding chaos. I have learned that establishing writing routines saves time in the long run and enables students to get to their writing more quickly. So for the first week or so, my mini-lessons focus not on craft but on classroom management. Those mini-lessons should be used to clearly explain

- where they should keep their drafts and finished work,

- how to use material in the Writing Center,

- what their options are when they feel like they're finished,

- what they should do if they want a writing conference.

Many school districts divide the school year into writing units and begin the year with a "launch unit" that settles students into the routines of writing. A two- or three-week launch unit allows you to teach the structures and strategies for the year ahead. In their book *Real-World Writers*, Ross Young and Felicity Ferguson (2021a) encourage teachers to start the year with a three-week Welcome Project.

It takes time to internalize any routine, but at some point writing routines will become automatic, almost invisible, for your students. We can see this happen in our own lives. At some point, when we refill the empty tray in the printer, we're not wondering how many sheets of paper should be added. Instead, we're thinking about what we're going to write next. We want the routines in the writing classroom to become part of students' muscle memory so they can focus on what's really important: the writing itself.

Freewrite & Reflection

Consider the following prompts. As you reflect on them, freewrite your ideas in your writer's notebook.

- What routines have I put in place to help my students write independently?

- How might I beg, borrow, or steal a few precious minutes so my students can have more time to write?

Create a Writing Community

3

The House of Writing gets built on two foundational beams: risk-taking and fluency. Everything follows from that.

—Ralph Fletcher

I was in shock. There was Robert, my fifteen-year-old son, on center stage at the theatre in Exeter, New Hampshire. Robert had joined the Oyster River Players, a local theatre group, and they were doing a performance of the musical *South Pacific*. Robert danced and sang, all the while wearing a coconut bra! The audience loved it.

I don't know exactly how director Kelly Eggers pulled it off, but somehow she created an environment in which an adolescent boy like Robert could take risks, put himself out there, and make himself vulnerable in a setting where he knew he wouldn't be ridiculed.

Creating community starts by creating a safe space. That's true whenever we venture into a new and unfamiliar world—sports, art, photography, ballroom dancing—and try to gain mastery over it. A safe space in the writing classroom is nonnegotiable because of this fundamental axiom: *Writers break easily.* Tape those words to your refrigerator. As writing teachers, it's our responsibility to actively monitor the classroom vibe to make sure kids will feel safe enough write.

Writers break easily.

"When an audience is safe you put out words more easily," Peter Elbow (1998) says in *Writing With Power*. "When it is dangerous you find it harder."

I visited a third-grade class during their writing time. One boy shared a sad piece about the death of his family dog.

"Oh how touching," one boy chirped, his voice dripping with sarcasm.

You could feel the chill in that classroom. After a snarky comment like that, nobody was going to get up and read anything sincere or meaningful. I wouldn't. The teacher met with that boy and made it clear that a mocking response like that would not be tolerated.

Writers break easily. It's your job to make sure they don't break in your classroom.

In *Welcome to Writing Workshop*, Shubitz and Dorfman (2019) say that a writing teacher's goal should be "to build and sustain a writing classroom community that fosters trust among students, and to clearly establish shared writing values about good writing, the work that writers do, and respect for each other's work" (p. 41). Trust, respect, and shared values are paramount.

Rico, a fourth grader in Portales, New Mexico, was a struggling student who didn't view himself as a writer.

"He didn't like writing traditional paragraphs," Amy Horton, his former teacher, recalls. "I realized that I was boxing him in with boring text structures and topics. At one point, he started writing his own movie script. When Rico was given creative freedom to be himself as a writer, he blossomed. The other students were excited to hear about the next scene in the movie Rico was making. They asked him to put his script in the classroom library. Rico wrote pages upon pages. He was so proud!"

Once his wri-dentity was ignited by working on his script, Rico created many pieces he was proud of, including this found poem about Martin Luther King, Jr. (see Figure 3.1). In this lesson, students were studying the civil rights movement and read the book *My Brother, Martin* by Christine King Farris (2006). Students were provided a copy of a few pages from the text to go through and identify words they felt were important to Dr. Martin Luther King, Jr. or his work. After identifying key words, students then cut out those words and arranged them in various ways to create a found poem. Then when they were happy with how it sounded, they glued the words down.

FIGURE 3.1   Rico's found poem about Martin Luther King Jr.

"The other students saw Rico as an author," Amy says. "More importantly, he believed that he was an author!"

I'm moved by many aspects of this story. Amy gave Rico the freedom to follow his passion. That was key. But I'm also struck by the unwavering support Rico received from his classmates. The whole class became Rico's fan club. They cheered him on. They reveled in his successes, and they were a big part in helping Rico to claim his wri-dentity.

In the world of sports, it's conventional wisdom that the home team enjoys a "home-court advantage." The absence of travel, familiarity with the venue, the presence of cheering fans, all give the home team a boost. We want students to feel the home-court advantage when they write and when they share their writing with the class. We want them to support each other just as Rico's friends pulled for him. The feeling should be *We're all going to live in this house of writing, and we're going to build it together.*

The Power of the Group

My wife JoAnn knits. Most of the time her knitting is solitary, but she has joined several knitting groups. Usually the group consists of a leader (expert knitter) and five or ten people like JoAnn.

Photo 3.1
Students work together in a small group on a writing project.

"I learn a lot, not just from the teacher but from listening to others," JoAnn says. "It's interesting to hear the problems they ran into, and how they solved them. And sometimes, when I'm tired and my energy is low, the energy of the group pulls me along."

JoAnn could have been talking about a writing community—learning a solitary activity by practicing but also by being in a group of like-minded people.

Healing a Rift in the Classroom Community

Creating community is not like throwing wildflower seeds into a meadow, standing back, and watching them grow. The classroom writing community won't necessarily take care of itself. It will require tending. At times there's a strong competitive vibe in the room, making it hard for kids to be generous with each other. (I experienced this firsthand while attending the graduate writing program at Columbia University.) Or perhaps there are competing factions in the room, pulling the class in different directions.

There's a fascinating segment, "Seth," in the documentary *Raising Cain: Exploring the Inner Lives of America's Boys* (Stern, 2006). The chapter features classroom dynamics in a kindergarten class at the Touchstone School in Grafton, Massachusetts. When Seth writes a story about an old man dying, the girls object. Several girls say it makes them feel sad when the boys write stories about death and dying.

Jean Katch, the teacher, listens as the class decides there should be no more stories about dying—only fainting. This new rule gets imposed, but it seems to have a negative impact on some boys, particularly Seth. We see him at his desk, listless, slumped over. He's usually eager to make a story, but he seems to have lost his oompf for writing.

It's clear to Jane that the new rule—no stories about dying, only fainting—is pinching some of the boys. So she reopens the discussion, inviting further dialogue. One boy suggests that a rule be imposed that nice guys can't get killed in stories. The kids like that idea, and several add that they don't mind if bad guys get killed. The class decides to implement a rule that from then on, the stories could be written with only the bad guys dying, but no good guys dying.

In the world of kindergarten morality, this compromise feels right— the good guys can't die but the bad guys can. The boys are fine with that. The whole class agrees. I have watched the Seth segment dozens of times. It's partly a story about gender differences, but it's also a story about creating community in a writing classroom. Jane Katch could have handled this situation very differently. She could have easily made the decision herself: "From now on this is what we're going to do."

But she didn't. She shared power. She invited discussion. And because kids had a genuine voice and were involved in resolving this issue, the resolution felt shared, communal. It brought that class closer together.

Fostering Helpful Peer Response to Student Writing

We need to teach students how to respond effectively to each other's writing. It's not particularly helpful when they hear from one of their peers, "That was good!" Young writers need to receive specific responses: "I liked the details you included when you described fileting the fish."

I've noticed that in many upper grade, middle school, and high school classes, students have trouble responding to writing without being evaluative. If you observe this in your class, teach your students how to respond to writing in a neutral way, using sentence starters like these:

- Your story seems to be about . . .

- I really connected to the part where . . .

- I wanted to know more about . . .

CHAPTER 3

This type of feedback gives the writer important information and lets them know what their writing has communicated. Notice that making a suggestion ("I think you should . . .") is conspicuously absent from this list. You might include it later in the year, but only after students have learned to give supportive, affirming responses.

The Place for Rituals

In Chapter 2, I said routines should be established early in the school year so students can be as independent as possible during writing time. But not all rituals in the writing classroom pertain to classroom management. Certain rituals can build and reinforce the sense of community in the classroom:

- **Thank the Writer.** Author Kelly Gallagher taught high school English in southern California. "Any time a writer shared a piece of her writing in my class, the first rule was we turned to that student and said, 'Thank you.' We did that to recognize and acknowledge the risk the writer was taking—especially adolescents who are all about *Hey, don't judge me!*"

- **Walk and Talk.** Amy Horton is a literacy coach in Portales, New Mexico. During writing time, she invites her students to stand up, holding any type of writing that they are ready to share.

  "When I say 'walk' the class begins to mix without any talking," Amy explains. "After a few moments I say 'talk' and they partner up with whoever is closest to them. I might do this two or three times. This allows students time to reread their work, share, and borrow ideas from several people."

- **Writer's Chant**. Rituals in a writing classroom include many small moves—two claps, for instance, after somebody finishes reading what they have written. But some teachers have found that larger, more dramatic rituals can be useful in building community. Katie Tingle, who teaches a transitional kindergarten class in Snohomish, Washington, begins her writing session with a communal chant:

> ## Let's say these TOGETHER!
>
> - I AM A WRITER!
>
> - I AM AN AUTHOR!
>
> - I AM CREATIVE!
>
> - I AM SMART!
>
> - I CAN DO IT!

"I've found that the chant sets the tone for the class," Katie says, "and reinforces the fact that everyone is a writer."

- **Writer's Pledge.** Grant Bearden teaches fourth grade in Kansas City, Missouri. At the beginning of the year all his students recite a Writer's Pledge:

> ## Writer's Pledge
>
> As I receive my writer's notebook, I promise to live as a writer. I will use my writer's notebook as a container for my thoughts, feelings, wonderings, and observations. I promise to use my grit and keep a positive attitude about writing. I will encourage and collaborate with the other writers in our room. I understand the importance of writing and the trust placed in me by my readers and will honor those readers.
>
> I know as a writer I MUST write.

"When we receive our writing notebooks we stand together and they repeat the Writer's Pledge after me," Grant explains. "I have it written out on chart paper and we each sign the bottom and post it in the room as a reminder of our 'responsibilities' as writers. I believe saying it out loud together helps create a common identity and community as writers. It reinforces the idea that we can all help each other out."

I asked Matt Glover what he thought about these big, splashy rituals.

"I think those rituals are fine as long as they're built on a foundation of what's happening day by day in the classroom," he replied. "But a chant at the beginning of the writing classroom can quickly become hollow . . . just like kids reciting the Pledge of Allegiance or the school's mission statement when many of the kids have no idea what they're about. If teachers are finding those chants or pledge to be successful it's because of what they do to back them up. I bet those teachers have writing conferences that are strength-based and encouraging, and I bet students look forward to them. I bet those teachers have a share time in which they celebrate student writing each day. You can get kids to say, 'I'm a writer!' But it's easy to crush that identity by what you do day by day."

It's a fair point. Rituals can be hollow and pointless. But a meaningful ritual in a writing classroom can bring the class together and reinforce the sense that we're in this together, and we need to support each other. Some rituals are one-and-done. I fertilize my lawn every spring and don't have to do that again until the fall. But establishing a writing community isn't something that will happen in one fell swoop.

"Creating a viable classroom community doesn't happen in the first six weeks of school," says Stacey Shubitz, co-author of *Welcome to Writing Workshop*. "Yes, those weeks are critical, but tending to the classroom community of writers is like nurturing an orchid. You must tend to it carefully for a long time in order for it to flourish."

Keep these principles in mind as you foster community in your writing classroom:

- **Open Admission.** Psycholinguist Frank Smith pointed out that teachers should strive to create a community of writers in which all kids feel like they belong. Everybody gets in. Everybody must be included.

"A true community accepts all kinds of writers, not just the 'best' ones," Carl Anderson adds. "Everyone's writing should be celebrated and seen as worthwhile."

- **Comfort.** Students need to feel "at home" in the classroom. Alan Wright worked in a classroom where two boys got excited about poetry. They met on the floor and worked on creating a poetry anthology during writing time. Their classmates nicknamed them the "Floor Poets." I'm struck by the teacher's willingness to let those two young poets use the classroom (in this case, the floor) in a way that made sense to them and made them feel comfortable.

- **Genuine Caring.** In their book *Reading Don't Fix No Chevys*, Michael Smith and Jeff Wilhelm (2002) make a powerful argument that students will only learn from people who know and care about them, value their evolving identities, and want what is best for them. They refer to this as the "social contract to care" in teaching.

Photo 3.2
Young writers thrive when they can create a community.

Be gentle with young writers and make sure they treat each other with respect. Getting laughed at when you share your writing can be a fatal blow to your wri-dentity, no matter how old you are. But if our students are met with support and appreciation for their efforts, they will blossom as writers.

Freewrite & Reflection

- Do I see my classroom as a collection of individual writers, or a community of writers?

- How do my students support each other as writers? What structures might I put into place to encourage students to be more supportive in this regard?

- Do my students respond to each other's writing in a way that's helpful?

- Are all writers valued in my classroom, or are some kids marginalized?

Build a Common Language

4

///

Language is a critical component of a community. Key terms could be a wonderful inquiry lesson: *What words and ideas do we all need to know for writing class to go well?*

—Melanie Meehan (2022)

I was brand new to photography. On my very first instructional photo trip I joined a group of people I had never met before. One morning I became aware that one guy was watching closely as I pulled a lens out of my camera bag.

"How fast is that lens?" he asked.

I stared at the lens, looking for some evidence of its speed, trying to suss out what he could possibly mean. How could a lens be fast?

I suffered through many moments like this. I found myself inundated by an alien vocabulary filled with strange new words (*bokeh*, for instance) as well as familiar words suddenly being used in a new way: *chimp, noise, prime, vignette*. The articles I read and the YouTube videos I watched referred to *stacked sensors* and *dynamic range*, baffling terms I didn't understand. In those early days, the lexicon of photography was a barrier I had to overcome. I didn't understand the terminology and, as a consequence, I felt excluded. At times I felt stupid.

I would eventually learn that in photography the word *noise* has nothing to do with sound. Noise is the grainy veil in a photo that obscures details. But grasping the specific meaning of noise, getting comfortable enough to use this word in a sentence, didn't happen overnight. It took time, but gradually I didn't feel like an idiot when I talked about *noise*, or a *prime* lens (as opposed to a telephoto lens), or *chimping* photos (viewing and deleting images while they're still in the camera). When that happened a door swung open inside me. I began to feel like I was a legitimate member of the team.

This phenomenon is true in any field: cooking, surfing, carpentry, pickleball, bodybuilding. The proper use of the lingo in a certain world makes us feel competent in that world. And it makes us feel included, like we truly belong.

You have to talk the talk if you want to walk the walk.

Identity is built on doing, devoting time to the activity, but it's also built on language. Being able to "speak photography" reinforced my identity as a photographer in several ways:

- It proved to others that I belonged.

- It proved to myself that I belonged. (Remember: building wri-dentity is an inside job.)

- It gave me essential language I would need as I delved deeper and, hopefully, became a better photographer.

In a similar way, our students must learn how to "speak writing." Writing is one of those subjects that can sound vague, abstract, floaty. If we want our students to grow their wri-dentity, we must make sure they're comfortable and conversant with writing. And we need to think carefully about what language we use when we talk about it.

> If we want our students to grow their wri-dentity, we must make sure they're comfortable and conversant with writing. And we need to think carefully about what language we use when we talk about it.

In my video *Dude, Listen to This!* a fourth-grade boy named David reads his story to a group of students. David is a verbal kid and a strong writer. But after he finishes reading his story to the class he mumbles hesitantly, trying to explain what kind of response he's looking for.

"And . . . should I edit?" David looks uncertain. "Like, wait, should I edit? Wait . . . should I edit a little bit?"

"You're looking for suggestions to make it better?" I ask him.

"Yes." David looks relieved. "Suggestions to make it better."

My language wasn't profound—*suggestions to make it better*—but David grabbed onto it. I think he repeated my words because they clarified his thinking and helped him grasp what kind of help he was looking for.

When we talk to students about writing, we use specific words. We need to define our terms and be thoughtful about what words we use. Language that's too esoteric (irony, tone, euphemism) may go over the heads of our students. But language that's too simplistic—a "hamburger essay" for instance—runs the risk of reducing writing to a formula that drains all the magic and mystery out of it. Skilled writing teachers look for Goldilocks language—not too simple but not highfalutin, either.

Our language about writing should include both process (*how* we write) as well as craft (*what* we write). Make sure that everybody understands the terms shown in Figure 4.1. Some writing teachers have found it useful to teach these words in a mini-lesson.

https://qrs.ly/pcgwtp4

Scan the QR code to watch the Dude, Listen to This! video.

FIGURE 4.1 Language About Writing	
PROCESS LANGUAGE	**CRAFT LANGUAGE**
Brainstorming	Lead
Planning	Character description
Drafting	Active and passive verbs
Rereading	Metaphor
Collaborating	Imagery
Revising	Simile
Getting feedback	Telling detail
Editing	Flashback
	Circular ending
	Hot spot (or climax)
	Interior dialogue
	Transitions

CHAPTER 4

In her book *Hidden Gems*, Katherine Bomer (2010) suggests various ways to find phrases we can use to talk about writing: our own reading, our own writing, reviews, the blurbs found on the backs of books. She also suggests paying attention to quotes from artists themselves.

A bit earlier I mentioned my conversation with a student named David in the *Dude, Listen to This!* video. After the class listened to his story and pointed out strengths in the writing, I decided to make one suggestion.

"When I write, my editors often tell me to watch out for 'echoing,'" I told David. "That's when I use the same word too many times. Go to the second paragraph of your story. You wrote, *The fog cloud came closer to the man. The fog trapped the man in its deadly fog.* See how you repeat the word *fog*?"

David nodded. "Yeah."

"I know if I did that my editor would put a little check mark above the word *fog* and write *Echo*. I wonder if you could you use another word for the second fog? What word could you use?"

"The mist?" he suggested.

"The fog trapped the man in its deadly mist," I said. "Yes!"

"Or . . . clutches!" David blurted.

"Or vapor," I put in.

"Yeah," David agreed, "since fog is just vapor."

Instead of using the word *redundant*, the writers in this class might start using the word *echo*—an authentic term published writers use when fine-tuning their work.

Having a common language will build your writing community and help students see themselves as writers. And in the most practical sense it will prevent confusion, such as when kids mistakenly refer to revising as "editing." There should be a shared understanding when any of these terms are mentioned.

But wait! There's more!

Language About Writing Invented by Students

Establishing a common writing language is important, but all the lingo shouldn't come from the teacher. Rather, the language about writing should be co-constructed by the entire class. When kids devise their own way of describing writing, using their own words, it becomes personal and intimate. It feels original, home-grown, and, I'd argue, it goes deeper.

In *Hidden Gems,* Katherine Bomer (2010) talks about Tiana, a sixth grader in Ohio, who was looking at a song in reading group. Tiana remarked that the writer was making a disguise.

"Songs use a disguise, like The Long Train means something beside a train that's long," Tiana said. "You know, like putting a mask on it and not saying what it really is."

"Tiana was describing a metaphor," Katherine writes, "but the other kids in the group instantly understood her idea about disguise, and that became the way that class explained when a writer is comparing something to something else" (p. 48).

Katherine also mentioned a student in her class who said, in reference to a book he was reading, "he liked the way the mountains were like a friend to the little girl; they breathed and they comforted her when she was sad. Even though he was describing personification, the kids referred to 'Daniel's mountain' whenever they wanted to make an inanimate object come alive in their writing" (p. 48). The key here is that Katherine paid close attention and noticed what the student said. She highlighted it and brought it forward, making it accessible to the entire class.

Don't be surprised if the writing language invented by students contains sly humor. I visited a class where Rachel, the teacher, was conducting a mini-lesson on the use of the apostrophe.

"When you want to use a contraction, you can use an apostrophe to replace certain letters," Rachel explained. "Instead of writing *I am* you can smush the words together and use the apostrophe to replace the letter *a.* That leaves *I'm.*"

She wrote it on a piece of chart paper:

I am
Iam
I'm

"Yeah, it's like the *A* dies!" Travis exclaimed. "And the apostrophe is like the gravestone to show where it died!"

Travis grinned, enormously pleased with himself. The other kids laughed.

"That's clever, Travis," Rachel admitted. "Very clever."

Of course, we still want students to know the conventional writing lexicon: metaphor, apostrophe. But the inventions devised by kids may be more personal, meaningful, and relevant to their own writing. A spontaneous invention like this—the apostrophe as gravestone—goes a long way toward building community in the classroom.

Envisioning Language

For several years my brother Joe has worked at the LA Food Fest. Joe is not a chef, though one year several chefs suddenly got sick and Joe got recruited to pinch hit. Before he knew it, Joe found himself in one of the Food Fest kitchens cooking a complicated dish. The kitchen heated up and things got hectic for a while. When the rush was over everyone let out a sigh of relief. One of the experienced cooks caught my brother's eye.

"Nice job, Chef," he said.

"That made me feel good," Joe recalls. "Like I was part of the team."

I'm struck by how that one word—Chef—could elicit that feeling and change the way Joe felt about himself as a cook.

"I always refer to my students as 'writers' in the lesson, just as I refer to them as 'mathematicians' during math class," says Amy Crehore, a fifth-grade teacher in Miami. "I believe this is 'envisioning language,' something I picked up from Responsive Classroom and *The Power of Our Words* [Denton, 2013]."

Several teachers have shared with me the importance of referring to students as writers (or even authors). When we address them this way we create a space that they can grow into. Doing so strengthens the writing community—everybody is a writer. The kids know it because the teacher says the same thing every day. It encourages students to see themselves as writers.

But I'll add this note of caution. Envisioning language by itself ("You are all writers!") isn't sufficient to build genuine wri-dentity. It's fine to refer to your students as writers so long as they have the opportunity to do the things writers do—write on a daily basis, choose their topics, explore their passions, write for real audiences. If that's not happening, if they're not getting to do what writers do, referring to them as writers will ring hollow.

Freewrite & Reflection

- When I talk about various aspects of writing, are all my students on the same page, with a common understanding?
- How could I expand my own vocabulary for describing the craft of writing?
- How could I make room for students to describe elements of writing in their own way?

Nurture Our
Own Wri-dentity

5

> We need to write with our students, alongside them, our pen frantically dancing across the page as we try to get our ideas on paper. When we write, and when we share what we've written, we show students a vulnerability that gives them permission to be vulnerable, too.
>
> —Amy Crehore, fifth-grade teacher

The fifth-grade class I visited was studying poetry. I gathered the kids and suggested one strategy poets sometimes use: writing through a mask, which involves writing about something as if that thing is speaking from its own point of view. "I am the grass, but people walk all over me . . ."

After sharing this strategy, we read *I Am the Ocean*, a book by Suzanna Marshak (1991), which provided relevant examples. I emphasized that writing through a mask was an optional strategy—"Try it if you'd like"—and sent the kids off to write.

There was an empty desk near the window, so I pulled out my writer's notebook and began to write. Everybody worked quietly for about twelve minutes before we gathered again to share. Some of the poems written by the boys were humorous: *I am the toaster, full of burnt crumbs . . .* One girl wrote a strong, angry poem that began *I am an island, floating in the Pacific, made up entirely of plastic . . .*

"How about you, Mr. Fletcher?" one girl asked. "Will you share what you wrote?"

I had anticipated that I might share my writing . . . so why did this question spark a sudden pang of insecurity?

"The Christmas season is over," I mumbled, "but I decided to write something about Christmas. Here goes."

> I once was a blue spruce,
>
> a real Christmas tree.
>
> During the holiday
>
> I brightened their house.
>
> My boughs held tinsel,
>
> lights and ornaments.
>
> But the holiday is over now.
>
> and I'm back in the woods,
>
> stuck in a snowbank,
>
> pointing straight up as before.
>
> No shiny presents under me,
>
> no lights or ornaments
>
> though I still keep the spirit.
>
> My branches are decorated
>
> with snow and icicles that
>
> sparkle in the moonlight.
>
> And I'm ready should some angel
>
> tumble down from the sky
>
> and need a place to rest.

After I finished reading there was a moment of respectful silence. A few kids nodded. Finally one boy spoke up.

"Not bad, Mr. Fletcher." He flashed a wry smile. "Not great—but not bad!"

The kids giggled, and I laughed, too.

Write with your students.

I could say this six ways to Sunday (and I probably will): The best way to build wri-dentity in the classroom is to write alongside your students.

Be a writer-teacher.

"I'd be grateful if you'd think of yourself as a writer and then as a teacher of writing," Mem Fox (1993) says in her book *Radical Reflections* ". . . and ask yourself when you or your students last ached with caring over what you were writing."

I'd be grateful if you'd think of yourself as a writer and then as a teacher of writing . . . and ask yourself when you or your students last ached with caring over what you were writing.

—Mem Fox

"If I were to give a tip to teachers, I'd tell them to take out a sheet of paper and start writing," says Jerome Harste. "I'd also tell them to share what they write with students. I think we (as teachers) provide the type of demonstration that students need to see and be around. There's power in making yourself as vulnerable as the students you're teaching" (quoted in Zumbrunn & Krause, 2012).

Write with your students. I originally planned to slot this chapter at the end of the book: *Don't forget to model yourself as a writer.* But the more I thought about it, the more I realized that positioning this chapter at the end would relegate it to an afterthought. This principle—the teacher-as-writer—is too important to bury in the back. This chapter needs to be front row center because writing with your students has so many benefits. Doing so allows you to

- **lead by example.** There's a huge difference between talking and the talk and walking the walk. When you immerse yourself in your own writing, you become one of them. They can see that you're taking the same risks that they are taking.

- **take the temperature of the class.** If the class environment is ultra-competitive or unsympathetic, you'll feel it when you share your own writing. The class vibe should not be *I want you to be quiet and write.* Instead, the message should be *I'm doing the same thing you're doing. Let's work together to create a supportive environment where we all can do our best writing.*

- **open up the inner dialogue that writers carry on when they're writing.** Viewed from the outside, writing looks private and inaccessible. That's why a writing think-aloud can be so eye-opening for students. *Should I add more detail about my cousin's*

> *Seeing me write in action allows them to understand the writing process in real time.*
> —Lisa Rose, eighth-grade English teacher

dress? Do I need to include a flashback that explains why she was so angry? This inner dialogue is invisible and inaccessible to students until we make it explicit.

"I like to write under a document camera and show students how writers tend to think aloud and rework their writing as they go along," says Lisa Rose, an eighth-grade English teacher from Delaware, Ohio. "Seeing me write in action allows them to understand the writing process in real time."

- **create a context for teaching about process.** "When we study published texts with our students we can find teaching points about craft," says Matt Glover, co-author of *How to Become a Better Writing Teacher*. "But when it comes to process teaching points, we need to examine our own process and share it with students."

Write with your students. That's easy to say, but I know from experience it's not always easy to do. My wife teaches yoga. She often reminds me how important yoga is in keeping us limber as we age.

"Even fifteen minutes of yoga in the morning will help your flexibility a lot," she says.

Fifteen minutes doesn't sound like much, so why do I struggle to do it? Truth be told, I'm not eager to add fifteen minutes to my already hectic morning schedule. Lazy? Distracted? The yoga mat stays rolled up. Yet on mornings when I add it, I notice that my body feels better all day. Change, even relatively small change (like writing with your students), can be difficult. Nevertheless, the benefits make it worth it.

Claiming Our Own Wri-dentity

It's a big step to go from "I do" to "I am." How do people cross that bridge and come to see themselves as writers? Every writer has a story to tell.

Nawal Qarooni (2023) was a newspaper reporter for years before publishing her first book, *Nourishing Caregiver Collaborations: Elevating Home Experiences and Classroom Practices for Collective Care*. I was surprised to learn that even after her book was published, Nawal had difficult claiming her identity as a writer.

"When you're a newspaper reporter there's no 'writing process,'" Nawal explains. "It's very much deadline writing. Impeccable accuracy is what matters. The writing process we teach kids—going back to writing, making it better, looking at another example, trying a different way—that didn't exist for me. I never had that kind of training. It's hard for me to see myself as a writer even though I was a published writer for many years before I wrote a book. I have hundreds of bylines that say my name, but because I wrote that that stuff so fast, under deadline (and often ended up throwing it in the garbage), I never learned how to go back and improve my writing."

Nawal had a solid foundation as a writer—she even had a degree in journalism—but that's not always the case. I know many teachers who initially didn't define themselves as a writer when they began sharing their writing with their students. But by getting into the habit of writing with their students, and sharing their rough drafts, they came to realize, *Hey, I can do this. My writing isn't half-bad.* They gradually built their own wri-dentity.

Sharing Our Wri-dentity in the Classroom

"The first responsibility of a teacher is to show children that writing is interesting, possible, and worthwhile," Frank Smith said, adding, "Teachers who are not members of the club cannot admit children to the club" (in Young & Ferguson, 2021b).

This truism holds for every field I can imagine. You wouldn't sign your kid up for trumpet lessons with someone who couldn't play the trumpet. I wouldn't go on a photography instruction trip if the leader wasn't a damn good photographer. The teacher needs to walk the walk. Let your students know your quirks, routines, and habits as a writer.

"I like to share photographs of my own writing places—parks, gardens, cafes, beaches . . ." says author and educator Alan Wright. "I show students pictures of my study where I am surrounded by shelves of books written by my author mentors."

Mike McCormick, who taught fifth grade in Eagle River, Alaska, shared a broader perspective on wri-dentity. He says that although sharing his identity as a writer was important, it was only part of what he wanted his students to know about him.

"I wanted to demonstrate that I was a literate person," McCormick says. "I wanted them to see that in my world, reading, writing, learning, sharing, talking, and teaching were all a part of a single fabric. If a student came to class and said she picked blueberries over the weekend, I'd share a poem by John Haines, or a passage by Alaska author Richard Nelson, or maybe the classic children's book *Blueberries for Sal.* I'd talk about my own blueberry picking experiences. Then I might suggest that picking blueberries could be a good writing topic for me and/or the student."

When I visit classrooms I often read appropriate snippets from my writer's notebook. I don't share my deepest and darkest secrets, but I do try to find something meaningful that kids can relate to. Sometimes I share an entry that's poignant—the last time I bought flowers for my mother before she passed away. Other notebook entries are playful or darkly funny: "When my son's fourth-grade teacher got sick, all the kids in the class sent her get-well cards. They were shocked when she corrected their get-well cards, with a red pen, from her hospital bed."

Every teacher I talked to affirmed the importance of the teacher sharing their wri-dentity with students. It seems like a no-brainer . . . so why doesn't it happen more often?

- **Teachers are chronically time-crunched.** They don't want to spend valuable time writing when they could be conferring with students.

- **Teachers don't enjoy writing.** In England, Paul Gardner (2014) surveyed 100 trainee teachers and found that only 1.8 percent of them write for pleasure. "Many enter the profession with negative views of writing and negative memories of being taught or learning to write" (Cremin et al., 2019).

  "Many people, even those with extensive educations, dislike writing, find it laborious, and feel they are not good at it," says Tom Newkirk (2023) in his book *Literacy's Democratic Roots*. "Most readers find their way to fluency and pleasure . . . but writing, sadly, is a different story."

- **Teachers don't see themselves as writers.** "Many teachers feel uncomfortable with writing, may not have a writing identity of their own, and because of their own discomfort avoid teaching writing," says Tasha Laman (2013), literacy professor at Western Washington University and author of *From Ideas to Words*.

If you are running into these obstacles, here are a few things to keep in mind:

- If you've suffered through negative writing experiences of your own, don't run away from them—face them directly. Write a personal narrative that reflects on your experience being taught to write. Your students will be interested in hearing this.

- If you're feeling insecure about modeling for your students, remember that being a writer (small *w*) is plenty good enough. You don't have to be a *Writer*. It's not necessary that you have published a book or an article. Show students how you use writing in your daily life.

  "I find that many teachers are incredibly resistant to sharing their own writing," Matt Glover says. "To help them get past that resistance, I try to assure them: 'You don't have to write this essay like a published essayist. You don't need to make this picture book like someone who does this for a living. And in fact if you do, if you have beautiful illustrations, that doesn't help your students. They don't need to see one more published text—they've already seen that. They need to see our approximations."

- If it feels like you're not doing your job by writing when you could be conferring, remember this: You're showing students how a writer looks, acts, and behaves. That's invaluable.

- Writing and sharing in the classroom will benefit your students and, at the same time, it will build your own wri-dentity. It's like going to the gym. Bit by bit, set by set, workout by workout, you can feel yourself getting stronger.

When you write with your students, don't just do it for them—do it for yourself. Kids will notice the difference. Writing with your students, and sharing what you write, can be humbling. Here's the reality: You may not be the best writer in the class! If you're teaching primary children, you're likely to be the top writer, but by middle and high school,

CHAPTER 5

you may well have students whose writing skills outshine your own. It may help to think of yourself as an *imperfect mentor*.

Teaching writing is akin to teaching a bunch of kids to swim. They change into their swimsuits, get into the pool, and start splashing around. You can see that some kids are already strong swimmers, but most are just learning. Some are afraid to put their heads underwater. It's tempting to stay high and dry, watching the action from above.

I encourage you to put down your clipboard and jump into the pool. That first jolt of water may make you gasp, but it doesn't take long to get used to it. Okay, so you're no Katie Ledecky or Michael Phelps, but your students need to see you stroking through the water, right alongside them.

Freewrite & Reflection

- What was one experience, positive or negative, that has shaped me as a writer?

- What attitudes about writing do I communicate to students? Am I passionate? Nervous? Indifferent?

- Do I think of myself as a Writer, a writer, or neither?

Promote Pleasure

6

//

> If you have emotions bottled up, writing is like a cage unlocked. When I write I feel free . . . like I can soar through the sky. My mind gets working and my body can't keep up. And let's be honest that's the best feeling in the world.
>
> —Emma Templeton, fifth-grade student

My grandsons go to karate class. The youngest has also joined a Cub Scout den. Both those activities include time for free play, but it's more than that. There are clear expectations for kids who decide to join these groups. The kids are expected to dress a certain way, act in a certain way, follow particular rituals. But the boys never miss a meeting. Why? What's the secret sauce?

Fun. If wasn't fun they wouldn't participate.

Fun matters. Enjoyment. Pleasure.

The same holds true for the writing classroom. Students need to enjoy writing. If we hope to build wri-dentity in our students, we must create classrooms in which they can experience the pleasures of writing.

Many researchers have affirmed this idea. In his book *Developing Talent in Young People*, Benjamin Bloom (1985) identifies having fun as crucial to sustained interest, engagement, and the eventual development of expertise when learning an activity. The research of Mary Helen Immordino-Yang (2016), an educational psychologist at the University of Southern California, demonstrates that emotion is crucial to learning. Students must care about what they're writing. Helping them find pleasure in writing isn't just a nice idea; it's essential if we want them to claim their wri-dentity.

But helping kids find pleasure in writing isn't easy because many students don't enjoy writing. And (as discussed in Chapter 5) many teachers don't like to write, either. Teachers carry battle scars from the way they were taught to write in school. Kids aren't stupid; when teachers bring their aversion to writing into the classroom, students pick up on it, however much we try to hide it.

I would never argue that writing is easy. Writing brings its pleasures, for sure, but there are difficulties, as well.

"I really don't like writing," one writer-friend admitted. "I like being done with writing."

"Writing a book is a horrible, exhausting struggle, like a long bout with some painful illness," George Orwell said. "One would never undertake such a thing if one were not driven on by some demon whom one can neither resist nor understand."

Okay, George, I wouldn't go THAT far, though I get your point. Everyone—even those of us who are passionate about writing—has wrestled with a difficult writing project at one time or another. Our students have, too. Many kids experience writing as a painful activity: *This is too much. This feels overwhelming.*

"There's a huge correlation between whether kids feel that they can (or can't) write and whether they enjoy it," notes Sharon Zumbrunn, a literacy professor at Virginia Commonwealth University. "It's difficult to enjoy things that are really difficult."

It seems like a vicious cycle: they're not good at writing, so they don't enjoy it, so they lack confidence, so their writing isn't very good, and so on. That's why it's so important that they have at least a few positive writing experiences along the way.

"If you enjoy something (even something tedious and mundane), you approach it with a different level of effort or grit or belief in your ability to perform," says Mike Reynolds, a literacy coach in Pennsylvania.

"Writing is hard, so if you go into it with the right attitude—if you can enjoy the struggle—you can get good at it."

Here are a few practical ways you can amp up the fun factor in your writing classroom:

- **Choice**. Elliott is a sixth-grade student in Western Massachusetts. I asked him to talk about when he gets enjoyment from writing when he's in school.

  "What I like about writing is the freedom to make my own story full of my own ideas . . . ideas I get inspired by from other books and movies and life experiences," he told me. "I feel most like a writer when I get to choose freely the topic, place, universe, themes, and characters instead of when I have to do an essay in school. I feel pressured when I have to write essays . . . my brain doesn't like to do all the planning. It's better when I can just free-write and then edit afterwards."

  The connection that Elliott makes (choice → fun/pleasure) is one that would resonate with many students. Elliott takes it a step further when he says he feels most like a writer (wri-dentity) when he gets to exercise choice. I explore the importance of choice more fully in Chapter 7.

- **Daily share time**. It's important to leave time so students can share what they have written.

  "One of the easiest ways to infuse joy into your writing workshop is to celebrate the work of young writers," Shubitz and Dorfman (2019) say in their book *Welcome to Writing Workshop*. "Celebrations are a wonderful way to provide students with an audience while acknowledging their efforts so that they receive the fuel they need to keep writing" (p. 51).

I visited a first-grade class and watched as a small girl took her turn to sit in the author's chair. She read her story to the class in a loud, clear voice. Then she paused before asking, "So, are there any compliments?"

The adults in the room shared an appreciative chuckle. I thought it was a telling moment: that girl fully expected that her audience would say positive things about her story. She was looking forward to those affirmations. That feels good. We'll take a deeper look at audience in Chapter 11.

- **Strengths-based writing conferences**. In her book *Reimagining Writing Assessment*, Maja Wilson (2017) asks teachers to reflect on what kind of demeanor we bring into the writing conferences we have with our students.

  "Do you present yourself as confrontational?" Maja asks. "Or do you present yourself as an ally to the writer?"

  "Students should be looking forward to a writing conference," Matt Glover says. "They should be fun! I never enjoyed a conference growing up because I'd think, 'Uh oh, here comes my teacher to tell me all the things I need to fix.' Which is very different than 'Here comes my teacher and she's going to tell me what I'm doing well and how to get even better at it.'"

  It can create management problems if too many students are trying to get your attention for a writing conference, but it's also an indication that they're looking forward to talking with you. And that's a good sign.

- **High-interest genres**. In my book *Joy Write: Cultivating High-Impact, Low-Stakes Writing* (Fletcher, 2017), I argue that too often students are limited to genres that are largely academic: essays, response to literature, compare/contrast, report writing, review writing. That is *not* what inspires young writers. Examine the many commercial writing programs on the market today and you'll be struck by the conspicuous absence of writing units that kids might find interesting: sports writing, poetry, graphic novels, comics, fiction.

  "Students need to be writing in high-engagement genres," says author Carl Anderson. "Too many of the genres kids are told to write in school are dull and not at all pleasurable to write in. For example, a literacy essay in elementary and middle school is an absolute travesty. The best I can say about being in hundreds of classrooms is that the kids are being compliant. It is not pleasurable, at least not in the way I find writing to be pleasurable."

- **Humor.** I visited a class of fourth graders. The purpose of my mini-lesson was to model for students how they might write about a member of their family. To do so I told them a story:

  One morning at breakfast, my seven-year-old son Robert barked at me: "Dad! Get me some cereal right now!"

  "Robert!" I glared at him. "Is that any way to talk to your father?"

  "Oh, right," Robert said. "I forgot the magic words—OR I'LL SUE YA!"

The class cracked up. For a full thirty seconds the room overflowed with laughter. No doubt Robert's remark was cheeky, impertinent, even a bit rude. But it was hysterically funny, at least to a class of ten-year-olds.

For their book *Reading Don't Fix No Chevys*, Michael Smith and Jeff Wilhelm (2002) conducted research with adolescent boys. The authors were struck by the boys' thirst for humor—and the lack of it in the language arts classroom.

"The boys desired to read humorous texts. . . . But laughter was never part of their school literacy experiences. In fact the boys struggled when asked to remember anything funny or humorous they had read in school" (p. 157).

Smith and Wilhelm's book has implications for all writing classrooms. By omitting humor from our class, we're communicating to kids that we don't value humor. And we're sending a clear message that we don't want them to write it. That's a shame because many young writers use humor to express themselves in writing. "Writing funny" is an essential part of their wri-dentity.

Want to bring more joy to the writing classroom? Tell a joke. Get silly. How about a unit on humor writing in which books by Dav Pilkey and Jon Sciezka are the mentor texts? Let your students try their hand at humor. It won't always lead to great writing, but you'll definitely notice an uptick in fun, laughter, and engagement.

Pleasures Large and Small

You can't build wri-dentity in a classroom unless it's fun and kids enjoy being there. Lately I've been paying attention to the pleasurable moments in my life. Small pleasures might include that first sip of morning coffee. A buttered slice of bakery bread. The feel of my favorite flannel writing shirt when I put it on. That stunning flash of cobalt when the male bluebird hits the feeder.

Writing contains many small pleasures, too. There's the pleasure I experience in finding just the right word to make a sentence work. A few paragraphs ago I wrote, "It won't always lead to great writing, but you'll definitely notice an uptick in fun, laughter, and engagement." In that sentence, *uptick* seemed like the perfect word. I got a small pang of pleasure when I used that word to make the sentence work.

My writing life contains plenty of large pleasures, too: coming up with a new idea, getting an appreciative note from someone who read one of my books, inventing a metaphor, discovering something unexpected through my writing. (See one such joy in the box below.)

When Bruce Springsteen appeared on *The Late Show,* he described the transformation that takes place when he and the E-Street Band put on a show.

"Before you go in its just an empty space, an empty building," Springsteen said. "The audience is going to come, and you're going to show up, and together you're going to manifest something that's very real, very tangible, but you're going to pull it out of thin air. It wasn't there before you showed up. It didn't exist. It's real magic."

Springsteen could just as well be describing the act of writing. I start with an empty space, a blank page or screen. I have to pull the writing out of thin air. It wasn't there before I wrote it. It doesn't exist until I bring it into existence.

It appears when I start to write.

Words. Images. Sentences. Story.

Often even I don't know where it comes from.

It's real magic.

Conjuring that magic is my most intense pleasure as a writer.

Note From a Former Student

Hello sir! I know you don't know me but I wanted to reach out to you and let you know that you came to my school in Brooklyn NY a very long time ago to read to us in the library. I wanted you to know though time has passed I think about your books often recently. I am about to be 25 years old and I have a 3 year old son. Being a parent shifts time and the perspective of time, it seems. I faintly recall in one of your books I think it was your memoir that talked about your grandmother or your mom (I apologize if I'm incorrect). I was about maybe 10 at the time but I recall her saving your baby teeth and planting them in the dirt. Like seeds. Nothing grew but something grew. You did. And I think about that a lot recently. Your books brought me great joy as a child and I hope one day I can introduce them to my son. I hope you're well! —Destiny D.

Freewrite & Reflection

- What aspects of writing do my students find most pleasurable?

- What small steps could I take to amp up the pleasure/fun in the writing classroom?

Give Voice to Choice

7

When you get choice in writing, you can express yourself in different ways and share your creativity.

—Bennett, fifth-grade student

Yeah, but when you don't get any choice it's like the words are stuck in your mouth.

—Emma, fifth-grade student

In this chapter I intend to tell a story. There's a protagonist, an antagonist, and lots of tension between the two.

But first a bit about me. I have been working on a memoir about my five brothers, the difficulties they have had in their lives, and how their struggles have impacted me. *Oh, Brother* is the working title. I've spent many hours on this project, and all the while I'm acutely aware of other, more immediate projects demanding my attention. I needed to finish this book, the one you're reading. I need to tweak the poems in *Double Exposure*, a novel-in-verse that I've got a contract for. And there's a manuscript I've been asked to review for *The Reading Teacher* journal.

But *Oh, Brother* keeps tugging on my sleeve. No editors or agents have expressed interest in this project. Hardly anyone even knows about it, but this story (a family saga) looms large in my heart and mind. I don't want to put it aside. The subject matters to me, so I choose to keep working on it.

Meet our protagonist: choice. Choice is oxygen to young writers. It's what they need in order to grow. Choice is essential in order for students to believe *I'm a writer*. In her book *The Dialectic of Freedom*, Maxine Greene (1988) argues that exercising choice allows a person to "choose oneself" and consciously mark their identity. The best way to help kids claim their identity as writers is by giving them the power to choose topic, genre, materials, the arc of the writing itself. Max, a third grader in Emily Callahan's class in Kansas City, Missouri, put it like this (Figure 7.1):

FIGURE 7.1   A third grader's reflection on writing choice

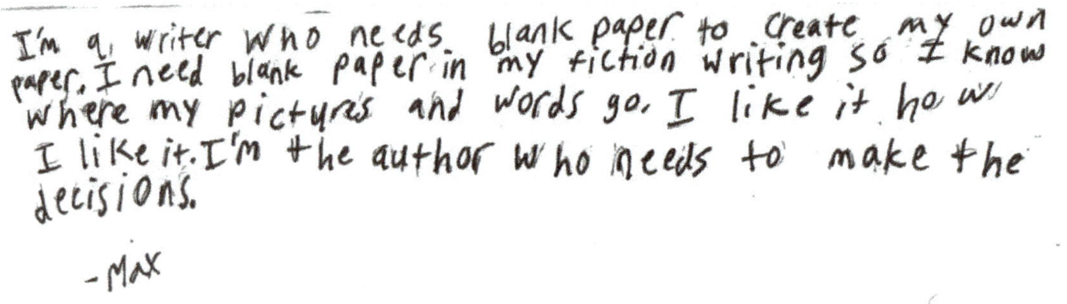

I'm a, writer who needs blank paper to create my own paper, I need blank paper in my fiction writing so I know where my pictures and words go. I like it how I like it. I'm the author who needs to make the decisions.

—Max

Aaron, a third grader, connects choice with pleasure: "Being able to have full control over what you write makes it more fun."

In their book *I'm the Kind of Kid Who. . . .* Debbie Miller and Emily Callahan (2022) embrace an expanded definition of choice that includes

- choice in material (markers, pens, pencils, paper, etc.),
- choice in topic and sometimes genre,
- choice in where to work.

Young writers need to make choices and live with the consequences. This shouldn't be a controversial idea. We know that students develop their reader identities by going to the library and choosing books by an author they love, in a series they love, in their favorite genre. Why should writing be any different?

"I have always used writing prompts in the past or made all students stick with the same style at the same time: narrative, expository, persuasive, descriptive," says Katie Tingle, a kindergarten teacher in Washington state. "But last year when I decided to give students a lot more freedom I noticed a huge difference. Students didn't want to stop writing. It felt so great! I did have writing conferences with each student, and we did eventually work on editing and revising, but we had built such a strong foundation that it was still fun!"

Choice in writing is inextricably linked to identity-as-a-writer. I interviewed Elliot, a sixth grader in western Massachusetts:

Ralph: How important is it that you get to choose a topic to write about?

Elliot: I feel like it's very important. One of the reasons I don't like writing in school that much is because we have set topics, set projects we have to do. I honestly just like to write my own stories.

Ralph: Don't you have a chance to do that in school?

Elliot: No. We did it once in third grade, and that was the best experience I've ever had in writing.

When kids can choose their own topics we learn about their obsessions: professional wrestling, football, gymnastics, hummingbirds, sloths. Moreover, we become aware of the "funds of knowledge" kids bring from home. Nancie Atwell (1998) advised students to make a list of topics they were interested in, genres they might want to try. That's valuable so long as students have choice and time to explore these writing territories.

Challenges to Choice in Today's Classroom

Choice, then, is essential to young writers. So what's the problem? Meet our antagonist: the recent wave of commercial writing curricula that feature a steady diet of academic writing. I have heard these writing programs referred to as "boxed curriculum," which feels like an apt description. They certainly box in teachers—and their students as well.

"There is a significant imbalance today between a constant focus on written response to text vs. original writing in which students choose their topic, audience and purpose and write joyfully to communicate something important to them," notes Ellin Keene, author of *Engaging Children: Igniting a Drive for Deeper Learning* (2018). "This problem has worsened since the Common Core State Standards were issued with their focus on close reading and response to text."

I don't intend to explore the pros and cons of commercial writing programs in this chapter, though I will acknowledge that some are better than others. I'm aware that certain writing programs do offer a measure of choice, though it's usually served as a garnish, not as the main course. These programs almost never allow students to choose their genre. Little wonder that in this more restrictive writing world, fewer children enjoy writing and perceive themselves as writers.

> When we rob children of the opportunity to explore a topic, try out a new craft move, or write across genres, we are depriving them of the opportunity to construct their writing identities.
> —Tasha Laman

"When we rob children of the opportunity to explore a topic, try out a new craft move, or write across genres, we are depriving them of the opportunity to construct their writing identities," says Tasha Laman, author of *From Ideas to Words* (2013).

This may seem like a problem with no solution. The protagonist and antagonist are at an impasse. Who blinks first?

Teachers, alas.

Teachers may be inclined to give their students more choice in writing. However, the commercial programs that the district has purchased—programs that must be followed with "fidelity"—don't allow it.

So is that it? Game over?

Not so fast. In their book *180 Days*, Kelly Gallagher and Penny Kittle (2018) identify choice as one of the four things (along with volume, modeling, and feedback) that make kids better writers. Many educators understand that there's no better fertilizer than choice when it comes to growing wri-dentity in your class. We cannot stand down on this issue. We can't give up on choice, even in this era where boxed programs proliferate. We have to find ways to give students genuine choice in order for them to grow into strong writers. Here are a few ways to do so:

Writer's Notebook

It's not a program. It's no more than a book consisting of blank pages. But the writer's notebook is a powerful tool—a high-comfort, low-risk place where kids can find their stride as writers. As I tell readers in *A Writer's Notebook: Unlocking the Writer Within You*, "A writer's notebook gives you a place to live like a writer, not just in school during writing time, but wherever you are, at any time of the day" (Fletcher, 1996, p. 4).

I've come up with many metaphors for the writer's notebook: a collection box, a playground, a compost heap, a piggybank to store ideas. But choice is a key element. Francis, a ten-year-old student, speaks to the importance of choice in the way he uses his notebook:

"I like to write about daring knights, beautiful princesses, ferocious dragons, trolls, tall castles, crazy foods, odd characters, peculiar places and anything else to do with fantasy. That's why my writer's notebook is special to me. I can write about anything, absolutely anything. My writer's notebook lets my imagination go free without anyone telling me I can't do that."

My notebook plays a leading role in my writing life. I use my notebook to sift a few jewels from the chaos of my daily life. My entries run the gamut from quirky to silly to poetic to poignant. One day my grandson Solomon was talking to his father, my stepson Taylor. Solomon asked, "Hey Dad, what was it like to switch fathers?"

You better believe I wrote that down.

I use my notebook to collect

- weird facts
- things I wonder about
- quotes
- memories
- mind pictures (things I see in the world)
- amazing descriptions I find in books
- "triggers"—ideas for my own writing
- dreams
- feelings

FIGURE 7.2   A snippet from my writer's notebook

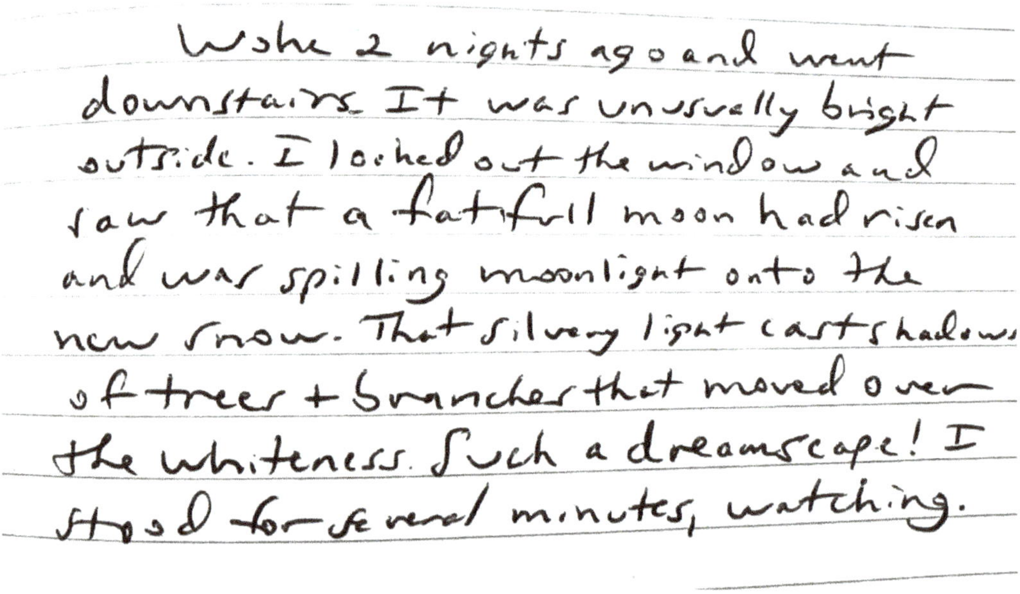

Woke 2 nights ago and went downstairs. It was unusually bright outside. I looked out the window and saw that a fatifull moon had risen and was spilling moonlight onto the new snow. That silvery light cast shadows of trees + branches that moved over the whiteness. Such a dreamscape! I stood for several minutes, watching.

Invite your students to do the same, using their notebook to collect words and ideas that interest, delight, or inspire them. In this era of restrictive writing curriculum, it's more important than ever that kids have a place for their personal writing.

Some teachers devote time the first few weeks of the year to introducing the writer's notebook and getting students comfortable keeping one. You might get them in the habit of pulling out their notebooks when they first enter the class, as a warm-up, or when they have finished an assignment.

The writer's notebook gives your students a way to exercise choice on a daily basis, to play with language, to build their wri-dentity in school and at home. In many classrooms the writer's notebook is featured at the beginning of the year in a "launch" or "living like a writer" unit. That's well and good, but when the curriculum moves to other genres the notebook gets left behind. "You should keep going in your writer's notebook," teachers tell students. But those words only go so far. Unless you're focusing on the writer's notebook (having kids share, sharing your own entries, etc.) it will languish, wither, and die.

Open Units

The writing landscape used to be wide-open territory. A teacher might opt to start the year with poetry, or memoir, or information writing. Today the school year has been carved up into discrete, predetermined units in which every kid is expected to write in the same genre at the same time. (Can you tell that I'm not a fan?) Some kids manage to do all right in this landscape, but many struggle and do not.

The reality is you may be expected to teach discrete writing units. Even if that's true, I suggest that you include two open genres, one at the beginning of the year, and one in the spring. By "open genre" I mean units in which students are empowered to choose both the topic and the genre. You'll see a palpable increase in energy, engagement, and laughter during these open units. Not only that, but you'll learn a ton about your student-writers.

In his book *Craft and Process Studies*, Matt Glover (2019) makes an eloquent argument for letting kids choose the genre in which they write. He makes a direct link between choice of genre and students' wri-dentity.

"This year in particular I've seen children's identities as writers change (and teachers' images of what children can do) by simply having a unit that allows for choice of genre at the beginning of the year," Matt says.

In Chapter 13 (Let Them Mess Around and Play) I will talk about "greenbelt writing," a concept that super-sizes choice and gives young writers total freedom.

Subversive Teaching

Choice is oxygen for growing writers. They won't get far without it. They won't come to see themselves as writers unless they have the opportunity to write about their obsessions and claim their writing territories. But, as we've seen, most commercial writing programs offer very little choice in writing. Is the situation hopeless? Can anything be done?

In her book *Becoming a Teacher*, Melinda Anderson (2020) follows LaQuisha Hall, a new teacher in Baltimore City. On several occasions LaQuisha engages in subversive teaching, telling her students they didn't have to read one of the traditional texts required by her school's curriculum and, instead, choosing something from her own library of racially and culturally diverse books. As a result, more of her students got excited about analyzing literature.

"This kind of thing happens in classrooms everywhere: smart, qualified, ethical teachers breaking rules, finding work-arounds, and flying under the radar to do things in a way that aligns with their expertise and experience, not the way they are told to do them," says Rebecca Gonzalez (2020), who blogs about education and reviewed Anderson's book. "These decisions are not made to avoid work or for the sake of being defiant; they arise from a perfect storm of knowing what your students need, learning best practices from educational research, and being stuck in a system where change comes slowly, if at all."

Our educational system puts a premium on teacher compliance and student compliance, but that's not the whole story. There has always been subversive teaching. There have always teachers bucking the system to give students what they need. It has happened for years and it's happening right now. I see these small acts of civil disobedience as acts of courage.

Sometimes you need to take a stand. Sometimes you have to close your door and do what you know is right. The district curriculum may not give students much choice in their writing. But if you believe your writers need a second (or third) helping of choice, I hope you'll give it to them.

Freewrite & Reflection

- How does having choice impact my own writing life?
- How much choice do my students have when they write?
- How might I give my students more choice, even in small ways, so they can find their stride as writers?

Confer With Students One-to-One

8

> A writing conference is a moment of being seen. When we sit beside a young writer, we're not just talking about craft; we're affirming that their words matter.
>
> —Georgia Heard

Your student sits at his desk. Maybe he's holding a pen or fingering a keyboard. Either way, the page is blank. The boy looks uneasy, out of his comfort zone. He doesn't exactly know how to begin, what to say, what words to choose, how to say it. He looks tense, and his mood doesn't brighten when you slide over and utter those fateful words:

"How's it going?"

The writing conference has a lot going for it. Talking to students and reading their rough drafts helps us understand who they are, not just as writers but as people. Isn't that what brought us into teaching in the first place? A one-on-one conference creates space for the student to tell you about her writing experience. You can point out strengths. You can teach a skill, not in isolation, but in the context of the students' own writing. It doesn't get better than that!

Poet and writing teacher Georgia Heard puts it like this: "A great conference is a blend of celebration and nudge—naming something the writer is already doing well so they begin to trust their instincts, then perhaps offering a next step to guide them in moving forward.

> A great conference is a blend of celebration and nudge—naming something the writer is already doing well so they begin to trust their instincts, then perhaps offering a next step to guide them in moving forward.
> —Georgia Heard

I always want kids to leave a conference feeling empowered—with a sense of possibility—rather than overwhelm them."

A writing conference gives us a rich opportunity to build wri-dentity in our students. You might be feeling overwhelmed by the idea of conferring with so many students. Entire books (by Carl Anderson, Patrick Allen, and others) have been published on this subject. At first glance, the writing conference sounds intimidating, but it doesn't have to be a big deal.

When literacy consultant Alan Wright asked young writers about conferencing, they invariably said, "That's when the teacher *fixes* your writing."

Uh, well, no. If that's how students look at a conference, if that's what's happening in a conference, we're in big trouble. I see the writing conference as a conversation between two writers—you and the student. It's an ongoing dialogue that will continue, hopefully every week, during the school year. A conference gives you a chance to listen, understand, and celebrate what the student is doing well. It's your opportunity to tailor your teaching to the young writer sitting beside you.

"Whole group teaching in a mini-lesson is efficient, but not as effective as a writing conference," Matt Glover points out. "Individual conferences represent the most differentiated instruction we can have. In a writing conference we're saying to the student, 'I'm going to teach you what you need, individually, right now.'"

Here are a few tips for conferring with young writers:

- **Be present.** "Attention is the rarest and purest form of generosity," the poet Simone Weil said. Attention is the most precious commodity we can offer a student. So when you confer with students, be present to them. We live in a world of distraction—tune it out! Our nonverbal communication—leaning forward, eyes alert—should reinforce the idea that we have come to listen. Our body language should tell the student that we are there for them. At the same time it should tell the rest of the class,

I'm conferring with this student. This time is very important so, unless it's an emergency, don't interrupt.

- **Be a reader before you're a teacher.** If you want to affect a young writer, let them see that their writing impacts you. That means reacting in a human way. Laugh if the piece is funny. If it's sad, let the student know you feel their sadness. Kelly Gallagher told me about a time he conferred with a tenth-grade girl who had asked for feedback on her story.

"It was a story about when she was in middle school," Kelly says. "She came home one day and found her mother was missing. Her mother had been deported, and the girl in my class had to become the mother figure for her two younger siblings. When she shared that with me there was something that happened between the two of us that was bigger than what was written on that page . . . something important that extended beyond writing."

- **Build on strengths.** Often the overall piece isn't particularly strong. That's okay. You can always find a section, a line—even a word!—that you can celebrate.

I conferred with Roland, a sixth grader who had written a poem titled "Girls." Much of the poem sounded rather ordinary to my ears (Girls, girls, always shopping for clothes . . .), though there was one line that caught my attention: Girls, girls, with finicky hair.

"I don't think I've seen the word *finicky* in a poem before," I told him.

"It means, like, fussy," Roland said.

"Great word! How did you come up with that line?"

He shrugged and smiled. "I dunno. My sister's always messing with her hair, combing it this way or that way . . . but she never likes how it looks."

"Finicky feels like the perfect word for your poem," I told Roland.

Build on strengths. You can instill a robust wri-dentity in your students if you do nothing more than highlight something specific they are doing well.

In a writing conference we're saying to the student, "I'm going to teach you what you need, individually, right now."
—Matt Glover

- **Keep it upbeat and positive.** What attitude should we bring to a writing conference? Do we want to come across as a welcoming host or a stern bouncer? This harks back to Maja Wilson (2017) when she asked teachers to consider a provocative question: Will I come across as confrontational or as an ally?

  Researcher Ross Young (2019) describes the most effective writing conferences he observed in England: "Their conferences were short, friendly, supportive, and incredibly positive. The children looked forward to them as they believed they would get genuine praise for and celebration of the writing goals they were achieving, but also good advice on how they could improve their developing compositions. This had a major impact on children's sense of self-efficacy" (p. 38).

  Matt Glover endorses that idea. "Students should be looking forward to a writing conference," he says. "They should be fun! I never enjoyed a conference growing up because I'd think, 'Uh oh, here comes my teacher with her red pen to tell me all the things to fix.' That's very different than 'Here comes my teacher and she's going to tell me what I'm doing well and how to get even better at it.'"

- **Treat every student like a writer.** In a conference, highlight how students are already embodying the identity of a writer. For example: "I notice all the juicy adjectives you included in your writing, just like Gary Paulsen did in *Dogsong*."

  Or, "I can see you're the kind of writer who likes to describe your characters so we can see them in our minds."

- **Keep writing conferences short.** Three to five minutes is about right. A long leisurely conference is a luxury you can't afford if you're trying to respond to a classroom of kids.

- **Teach one thing.** The writing conference is a time to support and affirm, but it's also a time to nudge.

  "I explain to kids that if we don't ever try to stretch our abilities, we won't grow," says literacy coach Mike Reynolds. "You weren't born knowing how to ride a bike. You had to make a decision that the reward was greater than the risk. Yes, writing can be difficult, but that's what makes it fun. I try to help my students feel comfortable being uncomfortable."

Skilled writing teachers watch and listen closely to figure out what the student is ready to learn next. They look for the *zone of proximate development*: the space between what the student can do independently and what they can do with the guidance of an adult or a more capable peer. The trick is to limit yourself to just one teaching point.

I conferred with Roxie, a fifth grader. She was working on a story about a family reunion.

"How's it going?" I asked.

"Well, okay." Roxie sighed. "But I think I've got too much talking."

"Too much dialogue?"

She nodded. "I think it's clogging up my story, kind of."

I nodded. "Here's what I do when I think I might have too much dialogue. I read over the story, looking for dialogue that's just chit-chatty, you know? I mean dialogue that doesn't really move the story forward. When I find that, I put brackets around it."

"To cut it?" Roxie looked doubtful. "I don't know. I mean, I'm not sure I want to take it out."

"Bracketing dialogue doesn't mean I'm definitely going to cut it," I explained. "It just means I'm considering cutting it."

"Oh."

"Yeah, and then I read it again, with and without the parts I've bracketed," I suggested. "I want to see how it sounds . . . how it changes the story. What do you think—could you try that?"

She nodded slowly. "Yeah, I think so."

"Give it a shot," I said. "I'll be curious to hear how it works out."

I tell kids, "You should be the best expert in the world on your writing." When I confer with students, I emphasize how important it is for them to reread what they've written. I might say,

"How do you think this piece is coming along?"

"Show me one part you're happy with."

"Is there any part you're having trouble with?"

In doing this, you're teaching students to skillfully reread what they have written. If you anticipate that your students will find this kind of self-evaluation challenging—and they probably will—introduce this idea during a whole-class mini-lesson. You can model this process with a piece of your own writing.

I tell students, "I can be a problem-solver in your writing, but it would be helpful if you're a problem-finder. Read it over and ask yourself *Where does it work well? Where does it need work?*"

- **Don't force students to revise.** If kids are going to see themselves as writers they must exercise choice, and that's not limited to choice of topic. Students should also be empowered to decide whether or not they want to revise. Most students only have a certain amount of "juice" for any one piece of writing. Once they're done, they're done. If it seems like a student has taken the piece far enough, don't belabor it. Let them move on to another piece of writing.

- **Help students think globally.** Writing teachers should always be trying to add to their students' toolbox. The conference is our opportunity to show students that a particular strategy isn't only relevant for this piece of writing; it's something they can use in all their writing.

- **Tell the story of your reading.** I'll admit it: Sometimes I draw a blank when I'm conferring with a young writer. I don't know what to say. When that happens, I find it useful to tell the student the story of my reading. Writers of all age can become self-absorbed; students need know what impact their writing has on another reader. Telling the story of my reading lets the writer know how their writing impacts me. It might sound something like this:

"I was intrigued by your topic—I used to do a lot of fishing when I was younger. The first few paragraphs grabbed me—all the gear you loaded onto the boat. I could feel a sense of anticipation and excitement. In the middle there was a part where I got lost. All these people came onto the boat. You give us a long list of names.

Some of them were your relatives, but I didn't understand who these others were . . ."

When you tell the story of your reading, you're not directing the student what to do. You're giving them information they need in order to decide what to do next with their writing.

"Conferences are invitations for students to assume an identity as a writer—or to deepen it," says Carl Anderson. "When we ask students, 'How's it going?' or 'What are you doing as a writer today?' we're asking them to engage in writer-to-writer talk."

A writing conference is a chance for precious one-to-one dialogue with a student, and it's a unique opportunity to help them believe in themselves as writers. But if we're not thoughtful, the conference can do the exact opposite and serve to tear down a student's wri-dentity.

"Depending on our relationship with a student, and the tone of the writing conference, we can support children's identity as writers or crush it," Matt Glover says. "My own children can even now point to specific elementary teachers from years ago who damaged their identities as readers, as writers, as mathematicians. And, they can tell you about the teachers who undid that damage. Unfortunately, teachers can damage a child's identity in a month . . . and it can take years to build it back up."

We should never forget that writers are fragile. They break easily, so let's be gentle when conferring with students. Tenderness is more important than technique.

Freewrite & Reflection

- Do I regularly confer with my students on their writing?
- If not, what's getting in the way?
- What is one of my bad habits in a writing conference and how might I correct it?
- What's a realistic goal for how many students I can confer with?

Use Mentor Texts to Build Vision

9

> Mentor texts serve as snapshots into the future. They help students envision the kind of writer they can become.
>
> —Lynne Dorfman and Rose Cappelli (2007)

During middle school, my son Joseph had Linda Rief as his Language Arts teacher. One day she read aloud "Where I'm From" by George Ella Lyons. This well-known poem includes these lines:

> I'm from fudge and eyeglasses,
>   from Imogene and Alafair.
> I'm from the know-it-alls
>   and the pass-it-ons,

The students read the poem. Linda gave them time to mark up the text, underlining their favorite lines. After the students got into pairs to discuss the piece, Linda issued a challenge.

"In this poem George Ella Lyons tells us where she's from . . . what things influenced her and make her who she is today," she said. "Now what about you? Where are you from?"

She gave the class time to write. Joseph's piece included this paragraph:

I'm from my 'Puff,' my very-small-now, but just-right-back-then blanket that I would drag everywhere with me when I was very young.

Lynne Dorfman and Rose Cappelli (2007) point out that when we share mentor texts with our students, the "fingerprints" of the author's craft often show up in our students' writing. You can clearly see fingerprints of "Where I'm From" in Joseph's writing. The poem by George Ella Lyons opened Joseph's eyes to a new craft move—the use of hyphenated words—he had never used before. Lyons' text gave him permission to do that in his own writing.

A strong mentor text will inspire students. When they read a superb mentor text it's as if some pixie dust falls off the words onto the students. Suddenly they're under the spell of the writing. Suddenly their writing toolbox has a new tool. They're surprised to discover they can write better than they've ever written before.

Teaching can be lonely . . . and teaching writing can feel even lonelier. But when you teach with a mentor text, you discover that you're not alone. When you read "Eleven" from *Woman Hollering Creek,* you look up from the text and are surprised to find Sandra Cisneros co-teaching right alongside you. Not bad!

Carl Anderson told me about visiting a kindergarten class that had been studying books by Donald Crews:

"The kids talked like this*: I want to write details like Donald.* Or, *Look, I did what Donald did"* Or, *You know, I think I wrote my book even better than Donald did!* I loved how the kids referred to Crews by his first name. It was almost like he was the class's imaginary writing friend, a writing avatar that they were in dialogue with. And because they saw themselves on his level, because they wrote books just like he did, they saw themselves as writers, too. I want kids to understand that real people write texts, and they can be that kind of person too."

Utilizing mentor texts in the writing classroom is a big subject. Entire books have been written on the subject. I've written one myself called *Mentor Author, Mentor Texts* (Fletcher, 2011). In this chapter, I won't go into detail on the particulars of using mentor texts with young writers, but I do want to highlight several important approaches for using mentor texts with your students:

- **Share published mentor texts during whole-class mini-lessons.** I encourage teachers to look for "micro-texts" that are short enough to be read in one sitting and lend themselves to rereading. In my book *Relatively Speaking: Poems About Family* (Fletcher, 1999), I wanted to write about how it felt to transition from a big family reunion back to your small, immediate family.

Shrink-Wrapped

We leave the reunion and go home
to a house that's way too quiet.

No more tag or kick-the-can or
killer-croquet with my cousins.

No more bloody war stories
from my big-bellied uncles.

No more staying up late watching TV
while grownups crazy-laugh in the kitchen.

Now it's just us. Boring us.

Our family suddenly becomes
like a package of plums
shrink-wrapped
at the supermarket

so small and tight
I can hardly breathe.

"Shrink-Wrapped" contains several craft moves, including repetition and rhyme. Students may also notice that the poem ends with a simile, a familiar one that (hopefully) most readers can relate to.

Reality check: Students probably won't jump at the chance to crack open a mentor text and harvest the craft moves found inside. This takes time. It takes talk. And it takes their active involvement. It's an unhealthy dynamic if students sit passively while we rush in, do all the talking, and explain what craft elements the mentor text contains. Also, you may share a mentor text with students that they're not impressed with. If that happens—and it will—don't expect to find fingerprints of the mentor text on your students' writing. Nevertheless, mentor texts give writing teachers a powerful tool.

- **Use student writing as mentor texts.** "Some of my most powerful writing units have been launched when we looked at how former students wrote memoirs, used dialogue, or slowed down the heart of a story," says Amy Crehore, fifth-grade teacher in Miami, Florida. "When students read the writing of a student they knew (or knew from afar), rather than a published author's writing, it's like a little voice whispers to them: 'Maybe I can do this. Maybe I can write like he did.'"

> When students read the writing of a student they knew (or knew from afar), rather than a published author's writing, it's like a little voice whispers to them: "Maybe I can do this. Maybe I can write like he did."
> —Amy Crehore, fifth-grade teacher

You don't necessarily have to share the entire piece. In fact I often find it useful to share just a section of what the student has written. For example, I had one boy who wrote a poem, "Jack-o-Lantern," that began with these two lines:

I love your uneven eyes.

How can I forget your rotten teeth?

This student had chosen a subject (Halloween pumpkins) that countless students have written about, and he had still been able to find a fresh way to make the topic come alive. I shared this poem with a class of fourth graders. We could have talked about the poem as a whole, but instead I asked students to focus on the surprising images in the first two lines.

Sometimes, instead of illustrating an element of craft, I share a student text for inspiration, to remind us of what strong writing sounds like. When Max was in fifth grade he wrote a powerful piece, "The Secrets of the Zoo." The essay muses on the reasons why a caged lion doesn't roar, and why many zoos must play prerecorded roaring sounds instead of the real thing. Max wrote,

Because the lion cannot roar. Or, more truly, the lion does not want to roar. So deep is its misery that he will forgo a gift that has been passed through his family for thousands of years.

This passage is eloquent and heartbreaking; it reminds me how powerful writing can be.

- **Share mentor texts you create yourself.** Kelly Gallagher says that creating our own mentor texts can break down the "wall of reluctance" in our students. But Kelly cautions that if the text is too strong, it can be intimidating to them.

  "You want to pick a text that will stretch them, but if it's too far beyond them you will lose them," Kelly says. "It's got to be within distance of what they can do."

  You may see this section heading and think, *But I'm not a published poet like Nikki Grimes or Naomi Shihab Nye. My poems aren't that good.* Good news: They don't have to be! In fact, it's helpful if the quality of your writing is closer to student writing than to published writing.

  "Teachers are often hesitant to share their own writing with students because they don't write like published mentor authors," Matt Glover says. "I tell them they don't need to. Students need to see levels of approximation. Our writing needs to be the bridge between published writing and student writing. If we write ours too well, then it's not a bridge."

  In Chapter 5 I suggested you think of yourself as an *imperfect mentor* for the young writers in your class. It may seem counterintuitive but it's true: It's your imperfection that makes it possible for them to learn from you.

- **Share mentor texts when you confer with students.** "I've found it powerful to use published texts in the research/discovery part of a conference," Matt Glover says. "When I notice a strength I often pull out a published text and say, 'That's so interesting that you used beautiful adjectives in your book. You know who else does that? Nicola Davies [2004] in *Bat Loves the Night*. Look at this page (I pull the book out). See what Nicola did? Nicola is just like you!' I've found this to be a powerful way to support identity when we help them see the connection between their writing and what published authors do."

I'm bullish on using mentor texts to build students' wri-dentity, with a few caveats. I'd caution against a heavy use of mentor texts because they will weigh down students rather than lift them up. I think of sharing a mentor text with students as akin to watching a how-to video on YouTube. The vibe should be "Let's see what this author has to say." But let's not belabor the mentor text. If it works as a springboard for students, great. If not, let's move on.

At the beginning of this chapter, I shared wise words by Lynne Dorfman and Rose Cappelli (2007) that when we share mentor texts with our students the fingerprints of the author's craft show up in our students' writing. I would add that mentor texts give us more than just a way for students to learn about the writer's craft. Sharing mentor texts with students can also have a powerful impact on their wri-dentity.

I did an author visit at a school in Connecticut. At the beginning of the day, all the students gathered in the auditorium for my presentation. They listened to me talk about the process I go through as a writer. I read snippets from some of my books and answered questions. Later that day, I was walking through the second-grade wing of the building when one of the students, a boy about seven years old, popped out of a classroom and immediately recognized me.

> "Mr. Fletcher! We read your book *Twilight Comes Twice*. It's so good!"
>
> "Really? You liked it?"
>
> He nodded enthusiastically. "That's like Shakespeare!"
>
> I grinned. How much could a second-grade kid possibly know about Shakespeare?
>
> "Thanks," I told him. "I appreciate that."
>
> "You got beautiful language in that book," the boy told me.

I caught the glint of admiration in his eyes. It was a telling moment because I think in his own way that boy was saying, *Okay, so maybe I can't do like you did. I can't write like that. Not yet. But I can hear it. And if I can hear it I can start building a road inside me. I can travel down that road. And someday—maybe not this year, or even next—but someday I can write something good, something I can be proud of, just like you did.*

Freewrite & Reflection

- Do the mentor texts I use lift my students up . . . or weigh them down?

- Am I giving students time to mark up mentor texts and to talk in small groups about the craft moves the author used in the writing?

- Do the "fingerprints" of these mentors show up in my students' writing?

- What might be the advantage of occasionally creating my own mentor texts to use as models?

Turn Up the Volume

10

Students need to read lots and lots of books. There are several contro-versial ideas in the world of reading instruction, but this isn't one of them. Most everybody agrees that volume in reading promotes fluency, stamina, stronger vocabulary, and independence.

The same holds true for writing. I reached out to a number of literacy experts who agreed that volume is crucial in order for kids to develop their wri-dentity.

"We define ourselves in this life by the things we spend a lot of time doing," says Katie Wood Ray, author of *Wondrous Words* (Ray & Villalba, 2025). "And to adopt an identity (as a cook, a photographer, a hiker, a golfer, a quilter, a gamer, etc.), we have to do the thing enough that we have all kinds of things we can tell you about *how* we do it. What our preferences are. Why we like to do it this way and not that way. What gear is best. What tools we prefer. When we prefer to do it. Where we prefer to do it. Who we prefer to do it with. We have to have stories to tell of the best and worst times doing it."

Katie's last sentence got me thinking; I had never considered the importance of telling stories in developing identity. Here's one of mine.

Andy Hunt and Steve Fishman were my best friends in Marshfield, Massachusetts, the town where I grew up. We had epic adventures exploring the woods, fields, and old barns on Acorn Street. At the end of my seventh grade, my father was promoted, and our family moved to Winnetka, Illinois. It was hard to say goodbye my buddies.

Over the next few years my family returned to Marshfield during the summer. I got to see my old friends a few times, but it wasn't the same. By the time I had graduated from college and landed my first job, I had lost track of them. Decades passed. I became a writer. I had no contact with Andy and Steve—I didn't even know if they were still alive—though their characters featured prominently when I published my memoir *Marshfield Dreams: When I Was a Kid*.

Photo 10.1 With childhood friends Andy Hunt (left) and Steve Fishman (right)

One day my phone rang. I immediately recognized the voice. It was Andy Hunt, my best friend who lived next to me on Acorn Street in Marshfield. Andy! One of our classmates had sent him a copy of *Marshfield Dreams*. Andy had sent it to Steve Fishman, and Steve read it too. We made plans to meet for lunch at a restaurant in Newburyport, Massachusetts. They were sitting at a table when I arrived at The Brown Cow. What pleasure to see my old buddies after so many years!

"Congratulations on your book!" Steve said.

"Yeah?" I laughed nervously. "You liked it?"

"It was amazing!"

"I didn't remember everything exactly as you wrote it," Andy said, speaking slowly. "But you definitely captured the feeling of what it was like to grow up in that neighborhood. You gave me back a part of my childhood I thought I had lost forever. And that's a precious thing."

You gave me back a part of my childhood I thought I had lost forever.
Does it get any better than that?

This story ends on a heartwarming note, though I could tell plenty of other stories that go in a different direction: nasty rejections, an almost-finished manuscript I left on a plane and lost forever, an angry parent who wanted to ban one of my books because it contained a poem she believed "teaches kids to hate America." Sigh.

> Stories are how we make sense of our lives. Stories are a fundamental way we claim our identity as writers.

Those stories matter, all of them. Stories are how we make sense of our lives. Stories are a fundamental way we claim our identity as writers.

On Writing Practice

What questions would our students tell about their writing? If they're not writing much, they won't have stories to tell.

When my son Robert was in first grade I said to him, "You're a good writer!"

"Well I'm not a good writer, not yet," he replied. "But I'm a good practicer."

It's an insightful remark because volume is really about practice. Students need to write—a lot—to claim their identity as writers. Annie Ward, co-author of *From Striving to Thriving* (Harvey & Ward, 2017), offered this insight:

"Not only does a predictable daily occasion to write offer a 'container' for kids' words," she said, "it likely influences their subconscious minds to generate, plan, and 'work on' ideas outside the classroom, in antici-pation of those regular opportunities to write."

Excellent point. If kids know they will be writing at a particular time they can be planful, alive to possibilities, during the rest of the day when they're not writing.

"The volume of writing is the key ingredient," says Kelly Gallagher. "If I provide good modeling, but my kids do not write much, they will not grow. If I confer with them, but they do not write much, my students will not grow. If I provide a lot of choice, but they do not write much, my students will not grow. Modeling, conferring, and choice are critical to growth, but if my students are not writing a lot, these factors become irrelevant."

I think of all the practice I have had in my venture into nature photography. I have an external hard drive containing more than 100,000 of my photos. Most aren't very good. Yet the time spent to take those photos made me feel part of that group, helped me put a down payment on identity in that world.

When you start to learn an activity, you get overwhelmed by all the paraphernalia and accessories. With time, and a great deal of practice, you start to get comfortable. When I started nature photography I was hyperfocused on shutter speed and what F-stop to use. I made every mistake you can imagine. I took umpteen dreadful pictures. But I learned by doing. Photography taught me. In time, my fingers developed enough muscle memory that didn't have to think about my camera settings. Now I could concentrate on whatever creature I was trying to photograph.

That's also true for young writers. At first they're thinking about rules: letters, how to spell a word, starting each sentence with a capital, where to begin a new paragraph, where to place the topic sentence, and so on. They need to know all that, for sure, but ultimately we want those conventions to become second nature to them. Instead of thinking about grammar rules, we want them to think hard about the subject of their writing.

Kelly Gallagher puts it like this: "If you hope to re-establish writing identity you need to re-establish writing momentum."

> If you hope to re-establish writing identity you need to re-establish writing momentum.
> —Kelly Gallagher

I asked Kelly what he meant by writing momentum.

"Getting words on the page," he replied. "Building fluency. If students are given ten minutes to write at the beginning of the year, many of them will only produce a few sentences. By mid-year, I'd like them to write a page in ten minutes. By the end of the year, two pages in twenty minutes. They are rusty as writers. I want them to flex their fluency muscles."

Quantity Matters

Volume is crucial in teaching kids about craft. "If you don't have many words on the page, it's hard to see possibilities for better craft," says Donna Santman (2005), author of *Shades of Meaning: Comprehension and Interpretation in the Middle Grades*. "We end up just talking about what more you can say, not how to say it better.

Quality matters. Of course we want to see strong writing, but when it comes to building their wri-dentity, the *quantity* of their writing is just as important as the *quality*.

Many young writers think big. They want to write a lot. They're eager to jump on the volume train.

"I'm writing a ten-book series!" a boy named Brian told me. "It's gonna be awesome!"

Later, when I conferred with Brian's teacher, she gave me a beleaguered look.

"A ten-book series! I know Brian—he's not kidding!" She sighed. "I'm trying to get my kids to write one solid paragraph. If they could do that—one paragraph!—I'd be thrilled."

I can relate to that. At our house my wife and I are involved in a major purge, getting ready to downsize, and it feels overwhelming. On some days I pick out a small area—the corner of a room, a closet, even one drawer—and work on that. That's all I can handle. So I understand that teachers feel something similar, the desire to limit the length of their students' writing. It's a matter of control and time. Yes, the desire to restrict student writing to manageable chunks is understandable, but it's misguided. Instead, teachers can encourage writing volume, but limit their feedback.

"What overwhelms teachers is thinking they need to read everything the students write," says Mike Reynolds, a teacher in Pennsylvania. "I walk around and glance/read over shoulders. Then every few weeks, I'll pass out Post-it notes and tell students to mark what I should read (and mark what they don't want me to read)."

Volume can also help students experience the pleasure of writing, as we talked about in Chapter 6.

"Volume matters," Michelle Rue says on the *Coach From the Couch* literacy blog. "Holding kids to only sentences or single paragraphs—and very formulaic at that—will only end up stifling them and will deplete their love for writing."

Here are a few strategies for increasing the volume of student writing.

- **De-emphasize prewriting.** All writers do some form of prewriting, even if it's just thinking ahead of time, or quickly jotting an idea in a writer's notebook. But we impose a burden on students when we require everybody to complete a formal prewriting sheet such as a web or story map. Most kids don't need it for every writing task.

  "Some students spend more time on planning than on writing," says Melanie Meehan. "By the time they write they are already sick of their piece. Encourage various ways to plan that differentiate and celebrate learning styles. Verbalizing, sketching, and acting out are ways that work for some students, helping them to visualize their story to completion. We want kids to be chomping at the bit to begin their writing."

  Many writers discover what they have to say in the act of the writing. It's fine to share various prewriting strategies with students, but make sure they understand that those strategies are optional.

- **Remind students of their obsessions.** I have written about growing up in Marshfield many times. The same is true about the car accident that claimed the life of my brother Bob. A rich topic is a well that a writer can dip into again and again. It doesn't get used up when you write about it once.

  Have students look through their writing to find those topics about which they have the most to say. You might say, "Gregg, I've noticed that whenever you write about hockey camp your writing seems to go on for pages. This might be a great topic for you to turn to whenever you're writing and need some fresh ideas."

- **Count words.** Don Murray carefully recorded his word count after each writing session. I used to smile at this preoccupation with word count, though I must admit that this habit has rubbed off on me because I find myself doing the same thing:

250 words—good start.

400–500—very solid morning.

750 words—stellar effort.

1000 words—heroic!

You'll want to adjust these benchmarks for what's developmentally appropriate for your students.

- **Allow keyboarding.** Many kids (especially boys) report that they find the act of writing painful. "My hand hurts." "I get handaches." Physical discomfort while writing impedes fluency and diminishes pleasure. You may find that allowing them to compose on a laptop or iPad increases their fluency along with the number of words they write.

- **Lower your expectations.** One day I met with several fourth-grade teachers; we discussed the kids' intense desire to write fiction.

"But it doesn't work out so well when they try to write fiction," one teacher lamented. "What they end up producing is pretty bad."

"I'm sure it is," I replied. "They're, what? Nine years old? Ten? They're just getting started. But doing that not-so-great writing is necessary in order for them to ultimately get good at it."

We can't realistically expect brilliant writing from a fourth or fifth grader. These students are in the early part of their journey to become competent writers. Early learning in any field brings a dose of wipeout and failure. Reality check: Students will create a lot of bad writing en route to becoming skillful writers. That's inevitable.

"The best teacher of writing is the writing," Don Murray said. In other words, students will learn by doing it. Kids who engage in regular writing practice get to make countless decisions about structure, craft, flow, and tone. They develop confidence and stamina. They find their rhythm as writers. They find flexible ways to solve the problems that arise whenever you write anything. They build their wri-dentity by mucking around in sentences day by day, word by word.

Freewrite & Reflection

- What attitude or stance do I communicate to my students when it comes to quality vs. quantity?

- What are some ways I could encourage my students to write more without it becoming a burden to me?

Connect Them to an Audience

11

///

The teachers whose classes did show strong writer-identities made a conscious effort for their children's writing to leave the classroom and for it to be published or performed elsewhere.

—Ross Young and Felicity Ferguson (2021b)

I read *The World According to Garp* when I was a beginning writer, and I was blown away. What a book! I wrote in my notebook: *I'd give my right arm to be able to write like that.* In full fan-boy mode, I decided to write to John Irving. My letter included an anecdote about novelist Caulder Willingham who taught one of my writing classes in college; we were all shocked when Willingham gave out cash prizes for those students who got the best grades in the class. I walked away with a cool $150.

I sent off my letter . . . and was stunned when John Irving wrote back to me! His postcard (Figure 11.1) earned a prime spot in my writer's notebook.

87

FIGURE 11.1 A postcard from John Irving

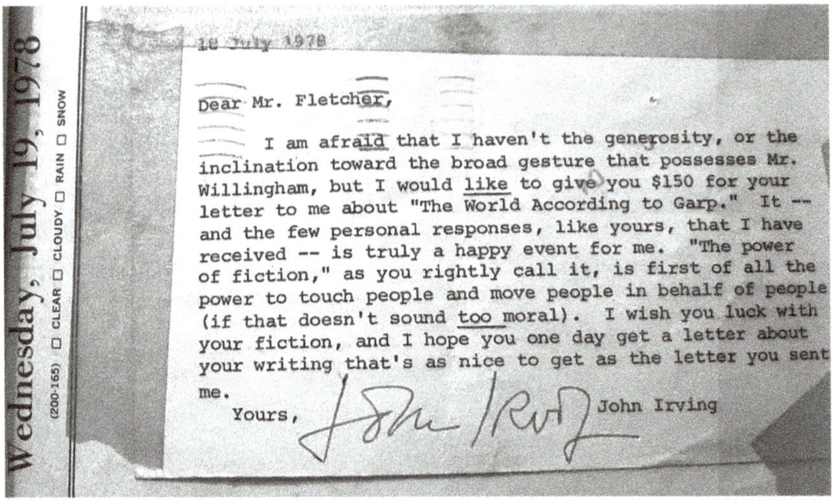

18 July 1978

Dear Mr. Fletcher,

I am afraid that I haven't the generosity, or the inclination toward the broad gesture that possesses Mr. Willingham, but I would like to give you $150 for your letter to me about "The World According to Garp." It -- and the few personal responses, like yours, that I have received -- is truly a happy event for me. "The power of fiction," as you rightly call it, is first of all the power to touch people and move people in behalf of people (if that doesn't sound too moral). I wish you luck with your fiction, and I hope you one day get a letter about your writing that's as nice to get as the letter you sent me.

Yours, John Irving

John Irving

A few years later I fell in love with books written by Cynthia Rylant. I got the idea to invite her to speak at a summer writing institute. I knew it was a long shot—Rylant rarely accepted speaking engagements—but I decided to give it a try. At that time, email had been invented but was not widely used, so I wrote an actual letter, in an envelope, with a stamp. Imagine that! And imagine my surprise when Cynthia Rylant wrote back and graciously accepted my invitation.

Later, at the summer institute on Long Island, New York, a teacher approached Cynthia Rylant.

"I know you don't usually make appearances," she said. "So how come we're lucky to have you with us this week? What made you decide to fly all the way from the West Coast to the East coast?"

Rylant smiled. "I liked Ralph's letter."

These experiences made a big impression on me. Writing wasn't simply a way to express yourself; it was also a powerful tool to get what you wanted. At this point in my career I hadn't published much of anything, but I learned that through my writing I could reach out to literary gods, figures who had seemed impossibly remote to me. Through the power of my words I got them to pay attention to a mere mortal like me!

Writing is often a solitary endeavor, but it can be more than that. At some point every writer feels the urge to "go public" with their work. I submitted many short stories, and got many rejection letters, until *Redbook* magazine finally bought one of my stories. It may seem shallow but it's true: Seeing my name in print in a national magazine was an important step in helping me see myself a writer.

I wrote poems for many years before my brother Tom and I held a poetry reading just before the Christmas holiday. This became an annual tradition, and it raised the stakes for me. I had my own opinion of my poetry, but I was always curious to road-test my poems, to see what friends and other writers would think when I read them out loud.

Anybody who creates anything hopes to find someone to receive their creation. Writers yearn to have somebody read their words. Finding your audience represents a crucial step in claiming your identity.

"I took up embroidery during the pandemic," notes Angela Faulhaber, assistant principal and former literacy coach. "But it wasn't until I finished a bunch of projects, and also started giving them as gifts, that I saw myself as a person who embroiders."

In the classroom we can help students find an audience of their peers. On many occasions I have seen the transformative impact that sharing can have on a writing classroom.

"One year I had a group of twenty-three students that was disproportionately boys—seventeen of them!" says Amy Crehore, who teaches fifth grade. "When I launched the poetry unit I was worried that they wouldn't be engaged. Boy, was I wrong! What helped them to get excited about poetry was the share portion of the workshop. Every day for five minutes a few students would share their goofy, clever, or poignant poems, and the grins on their faces were priceless. They definitely saw themselves as writers!"

Amy's experience affirms something about audience I wrote in my book *Boy Writers: Reclaiming Their Voices*: Girls write for the teacher, but boys write for each other (Fletcher, 2006). No generalization holds true all the time, but there's a nugget of truth here.

CHAPTER 11

Tasha Laman is a literacy professor at Western Washington University. "We had an author celebration in a third-grade room where the children are not typically engaged in a writing workshop model," Tasha says. "The children read their memoirs to a small group of peers, and then we had a 'museum share' where the children read each other's memoirs and responded in little booklets. At the end of the celebration, I asked the children what they thought. One little boy raised his hand and said, 'I'm so proud of all of us. We all shared with each other, and now we know things about each other that we didn't know.'"

When kids know that their writing will have a real audience, they'll work harder at it. They will understand the importance of correct punctuation and spelling. Most important, they get to see the impact that their words can have.

Unfortunately, the share session seems to be disappearing in classrooms dominated by test prep, writing about reading, and so on. That's unfortunate because audience is a crucial ingredient in wri-dentity. In this chapter, we'll examine various kinds of sharing opportunities and practical ways to help young writers connect with an authentic audience.

- **Sharing with yourself**. Wait, what? Sharing with yourself? Isn't the whole idea of audience to bring your writing from yourself out to the larger world?

  Well, yes and no. I will always be my own first audience, the first person I write for. I write to please myself because I know I'm not much different from other readers. If I like a sentence, phrase, or description I have written, I figure a phantom reader might like it, too. If it sounds trite to me, I know there's a very good chance that reader will experience it the same way.

  I tell kids, "When it comes to your writing, you need to be the best expert in the world." Skilled writers are both writers and critics. We write a sentence or paragraph, and then we stand back, reread, and decide if it's any good. I encourage students to read their pieces and note the parts that work well. But I also want them to think about how they might improve, or cut, the parts that don't.

- **Sharing with the teacher in a conference.** "Writing is about having an audience," Matt Glover says, "and the teacher in a writing

CHAPTER 11

conference is the child's first audience for a piece of writing—though hopefully not the last."

In Chapter 8 we talked about creating a positive vibe in these conferences, highlighting the positives, being an ally to the young writer. When you think about it, it's a privilege to be the first one to receive a piece of writing. We should respond with a feeling of respect and appreciation for the students' efforts.

> Writing is about having an audience, and the teacher in a writing conference is the child's first audience for a piece of writing—though hopefully not the last. —Matt Glover

- **Sharing with a writing partner.** Although I'm bullish on the whole-class share, I'll admit that it's not a very efficient way to provide an audience for students because it can take a long time before everybody has a chance to share in front of the class. For this reason, smaller share groups are invaluable. In *Welcome to Writing Workshop*, Stacey Shubitz and Lynne Dorfman (2019) describe "writing partnerships," in which every student has a designated share partner. "We think it's important to implement writing partnerships during the first weeks of the school year," they say. "It doesn't matter if your students are new to one another or have known one another for years."

  "In classrooms that have strong partnerships in place, this is such a great way to get kids to think about how their writing lands with a reader in a low stakes way," says Gina Dignon, a literacy coach. "Strong partnerships can help students throughout the writing process."

- **Sharing with the whole class.** Students look forward to the opportunity to sit in the author's chair, have the attention of the entire class, and share what they've written. The whole-class share session offers us a great way to cement the community in the classroom and to build wri-dentity in students sharing their work. A few points to remember:

  The writer is in charge. The writer should let the class know what kind of help they need:

  - Does it make sense?
  - Have I left anything out?
  - Can you picture what's going on?

With older students, consider having kids make brief written—as opposed to verbal—response. Each student gets a small index card and writes a brief note to the author. The responders should be coached to be specific, positive, and to address the help the author asked for.

Monitor the feel of the room when kids share their writing. I've been in classrooms where the vibe was highly competitive, almost hostile. It felt adversarial, like lawyers cross-examining a witness, when other students responded to the writer. An atmosphere like that will not bolster wri-dentity.

- **Sharing personal writing projects**. Giving writing to another person is like giving blood—it comes from the heart of the writer to the heart of the reader.

"I feel most like a writer when I get to use my writing knowledge and skills," says Kalina, an eighth-grade student. "For instance, a close friend of mine's birthday is coming up, and I chose to write a poem to show my appreciation towards her."

In Emily Callahan's class, one student, Ruby, wrote a book about how to handle big feelings (Figure 11.2), but she took it a step

FIGURE 11.2   The cover of Ruby's book

further than just writing it. Ruby asked Emily to make copies of her book for other teachers and suggested they could put her book in the "calming corners" of their classrooms.

Students should be encouraged to find the appropriate audience for their writing. In a writing conference, we might ask, "Have you thought about what you might want to do with this writing? Who do you think would really love to read this?"

- **Share with the community.** Ellen Ervin taught elementary and middle school in the school district where my kids went to school. One year she and her fourth-grade class wrote a field guide to the flora and fauna around the schoolyard at Moharimet Elementary school.

  "The students wrote the text for each entry," Ellen says. "We used only photos and illustrations from our school community (my students, teachers, parents, alumni, and grandparents). We had our field guide checked for accuracy by six professors and published hundreds of copies. We sold them for $6 at our pancake breakfast and out of the office that year. We made around $1000 and put the money towards outdoor programs at school. Now, years later, the books are still used for research in all the classrooms. When a fourth-grade class was doing research this fall for fictional stories about the forest, the teacher requested a set of our field guides rather than taking any books out of the library. I love seeing how this project has such a long-lasting impact and large audience."

  In her last sentence, Ellen is referring to the impact those field guides had on the public. But this experience surely had a profound effect on the kids who created them. Ellen's students saw the many tangible ways their finished work rippled out into the world. An experience like that is a sure-fire way to build wri-dentity.

- **Going public to shake things up.** Writing enables us to lift our voices, to shape the kind of world we want to live in. And it can be a way to challenge the power structure. My book *A Writer's Notebook* includes a chapter titled "Use Writing to Rock Your World." I describe *The Bloodthirsty Wolverine*, an underground newspaper created by my sisters and friends in high school. I also mention Chris Hass, a teacher in South Carolina. He and his students noticed that nearly every street in Columbia was named after prominent men. But what about the prominent women who had played an important role in Columbia's history? The students decided to do something about it. They began writing letters to the Columbia City Council. Some of the kids visited the Council to read the letters out loud. The letters worked. The city renamed one of the streets after Dr. Matilda Evans, the first Black woman licensed to practice medicine in South Carolina.

- **Celebration**. "Celebrations infuse joy into the classroom," Stacey Shubitz says. A writing celebration can be a quiet event—nothing wrong with that—but there's also a place for a big, splashy event designed to get everybody's attention and give students the widest audience possible for their writing.

Melanie Meehan has seen classrooms with shares modeled after the popular TV show *The Voice*. In this competition, students audition by submitting one paragraph of their writing that is read aloud by someone else. A panel of student judges look away from the reader so they can concentrate on the quality of the writing. They "turn their chairs," or don't, depending on the quality of the writing.

Sara Tillett, a middle school teacher, came up with a novel way for her eighth-grade students to share their writing. "Eighth graders are kids who love the dramatic flair," Sara says. "Being over the top is what they need to make something memorable. So I came up with Funeral for a Bad Word. The kids picked out a word and wrote about it. On the day of the funeral the kids all wore black. Funny: They never remember to bring their pencils,

Photo 11.1
Funeral for a word

but on that day they remembered to wear all black. Some kids wore suits and long gloves. Each class had two to four students read aloud a eulogy. They pretended to cry. I split the funeral into the service and then a therapy session where they each rewrote a paragraph that contained the words. The following day, they scoured their essays for the 'bad words' to remove them."

I didn't get to witness this funeral, but Sara's description helped me picture it. This event had everything that would appeal to an adolescent: drama, theater, fashion, and plenty of humor. Figure 11.3 offers an example of writing that was shared that day.

FIGURE 11.3   Word Eulogy

by Vivi and Ruby

We're here today to mourn the loss of some words that we all held very close to our hearts. The first word that we have lost today is Totally. I have many cherished memories with Totally. I still remember when, years ago, totally was everyone's favorite word. He was loved by many and used all the time. People used Totally in lots of different sentences. He was truly a big part of people's writing and reading. Never again will we hear people say they "totally want to do something", or that something "totally happened". Although Totally was used in many people's conversations, he was also strong and independent, sometimes showing up as a single word response to a question. Totally had three syllables and a double L. Totally was an extremely agreeable word who had a way of making people feel like they were cool. He was always able to see the best in people. Totally was never negative and was always enthusiastic about the topic he was talking about. We are deeply saddened to lose the use of Totally in our vocabulary. He will be forever missed by all of his friends and family.

Freewrite & Reflection

- Do my students have small and big ways to share their writing?

- How do whole-class share sessions impact students when they share their work?

- How could I help students connect with a wider audience for their writing?

Give "Never-Writers" a Fresh Start

12

Certain kids just need a fail-free place to write next to powerful words from others that give them courage . . . plus the volume of practice to make writing less scary.

—Penny Kittle

"I'm not a writer."

"I don't like to write."

"I hate writing!"

You know these kids, the ones who are quick to give writing a big thumbs down. You've had them in class. They might even be your own children. They've been labeled "reluctant writers," but that doesn't tell the whole story. These students proudly identify as "never-writers." Although they don't all share the same story or history, it's a good bet they've each had some bad writing experiences. That's true for most people. They carry invisible writing scars, usually from a particular adult or teacher who was overly critical.

In this chapter, I want to look at some ways we might handle those kids with negative wri-dentity. Spoiler alert: There are no easy answers. It's unrealistic to think we can instantly transform those naysayers into kids who suddenly love writing. But we can find ways to crack open the door so those students are willing to give writing—and themselves as writers—a fighting chance.

The drawings in this chapter were created by students in a public school in New Mexico. I got the idea from a similar study conducted by educational researcher Sharon Zumbrunn and colleagues (2017). Inspired by the Zumbrunn et al. study, my colleague Amy Horton invited students to "draw a picture about a recent experience you had with writing and how that experience made you feel." After finishing their drawings, the students were asked to respond to this prompt: "What did you draw? Use the back of this paper to write a description for your drawing."

FIGURE 12.1   A student drawing responding to the prompt "draw a picture about a recent experience you had with writing and how that experience made you feel." The student explained, "I drew this picture of crying because I get bullied for how bad I write. Writing makes me sad. It also makes me sad because it hurts my fingers and I prefer to type."

Overall the student drawings conveyed a range of emotions: joy, apathy, anxiety, frustration, and unhappiness. The majority of kids created drawings that expressed a positive outlook on writing, but not everybody. The drawings included in this chapter (Figures 12.1–12.3 and Figures 12.5–12.6) show a number of students with a negative wri-dentity. I was struck by how details in the drawings—facial expressions, the distance between student and teacher—provided insight into their attitudes toward writing. As you read and look at the drawings, reflect on what the drawings say about how each student felt about writing and what kind of art the students in your class might produce.

> FIGURE 12.2   When asked to draw and write about their experience with writing, this student wrote "I don't like writing because it makes MY FINGERS HURT. The top picture is from a third person POV. The second picture is from a first person POV. The pencil is supposed to represent writing and the symbols are supposed to represent my negative feelings about it."

Meet the Never-Writer

Kids who dislike writing aren't rare. You'll probably have one in your class this year; in fact, you'll be lucky if you only have one! It may be tempting to write off kids like that—*not every kid is going to like every subject*—but I don't think that's wise. The number of these anti-writers may be small, but their aversion to writing is a burden to them and a serious impediment to their intellectual growth. They're going to need to learn how to write! You can't get very far without it.

Sometimes *I'm-not-a-writer* becomes its own kind of identity, a defiant badge kids wear with pride. I have found that students who proclaim that they hate writing often have an outsized influence on the tenor of your class, especially if they are popular, funny, or talented athletes.

I talked with a number of teachers and literacy leaders who shared their best advice and strategies for how to respond to students like that. Matt Glover worked with a non-writer named Connor, while doing some demonstration teaching. During that class Matt decided to do everything possible to impact Connor's confidence and identity as a writer:

- He called on Connor during the mini-lesson: "Connor, what would you do . . . ?"

- When Matt conferred with him, he compared Connor's writing to a work by a published author. "Oh, you're just like Gail Gibbons . . ."

- He was careful to choose just one small teaching point during his conference with Connor. He didn't want to overwhelm him with suggestions.

- When he conferred with another student, he used Connor's writing as a mentor text. "Jamie, let me show you what Connor did . . ."

- He featured Connor's writing during share time.

"Normally I wouldn't do all of these things with Connor in one class," Matt says. "But if we could do just one of them each day we could start to impact Connor's engagement and identity as a writer."

FIGURE 12.3   When asked to draw and reflect on his experience with writing, this third-grade student wrote, "I drew me doing a paper. I feel upset and bored and tired."

Here are other practical strategies for dealing with students who see themselves as non-writers.

- **Address them as writers.** It's important to address all your students as writers—not just the best writers—and make sure to include the anti-writers when you do so. As stated in Chapter 7, referring to your students as writers may seem superficial, but it's an example of "envisioning language," offering them an identity to grow into.

- **Invite them to make an identity web (Figure 12.4).** Gina Dignon has worked as a teacher and literacy coach for twenty years. I asked her how she deals with students who have a negative wri-dentity.

"I try to get to know kids in different ways: their interests outside of school, what they enjoy doing, where they are from, their families, etc.," Gina says. "I have had some luck in sharing my own identity web (based on Sara Ahmed's [2018] *Being the Change*, or using a picture book like *What I Am* by Divya Srinivasan [2021]) to get students to reflect and create their own web. They can then use one of those topics to start writing."

FIGURE 12.4   Sample identity web

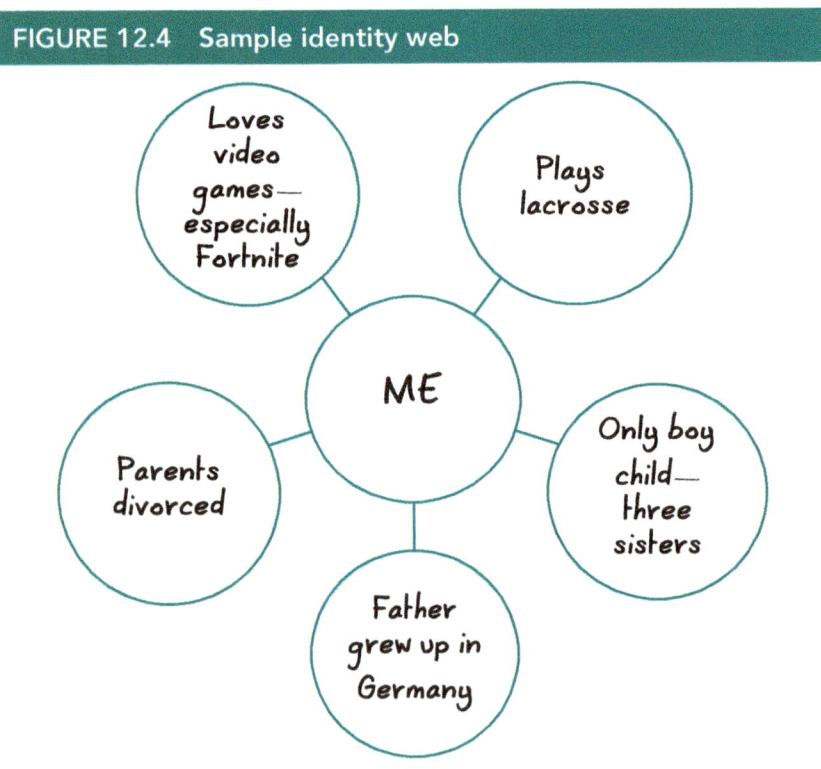

- **Give freedom through choice.** I have noticed that reluctant writers often get *too much* scaffolding: webs, rubrics, and so on. You might think all that "help" would make it easier for them to write, but it doesn't. I suggest going in the opposite direction. Give those kids more freedom, more choice.

"This fall I told students the first assignment could be any genre," Penny Kittle told me about working with her high schoolers. "I had one caveat: to tell a story—fiction or nonfiction, it didn't matter. But story skills did. That released them from the pressure and competition of those rubrics and 'expectations' that tell kids exactly what it must be.

"[One student] Matt told me he just couldn't figure out what to write. He was frustrated. In the conference I asked, 'So what else are you thinking about?'

"He looked at me—like, honestly? 'Well, my brother's wedding is this weekend. I'm the best man and I have to write a speech.'

"So he worked on that speech," Penny says. "And the next week he revised it because everyone wanted a copy, and he wanted to make it better."

- **Puke out the writing**. Sara Tillett tells her middle school students to "puke out" their writing. She has found that using this colorful verb highlights the fact that first drafts are often dreadful.

  "I want them to write their worst piece," she says. "Kids get hung up on being perfect, producing a piece they don't need to redraft, writing that will make their teacher happy. Then, all too often, they stare at a blank page and get seized by anxiety because they can't do it perfectly. I tell them to puke and then look for the good or the gold nuggets. If they focus on making it their worst draft, they will get something of value without being caught in the perfect."

- **Let them draw.** Many teachers allow drawing for primary students but outlaw it with older students. That's a mistake. Drawing is a comfort zone for many kids (especially boys). We may see drawing as wasted time, or writing avoidance, but in fact the time they spend drawing gives them an opportunity to brainstorm what they're going to write. We can use graphic novels as mentor texts to show that many writers use drawings coupled with text to tell a story.

Kids get hung up on being perfect, producing a piece they don't need to redraft, writing that will make their teacher happy. Then, all too often, they stare at a blank page and get seized by anxiety because they can't do it perfectly. I tell them to puke and then look for the good or the gold nuggets. If they focus on making it their worst draft, they will get something of value without being caught in the perfect.
—Sara Tillett, eighth-grade teacher

CHAPTER 12

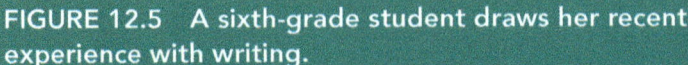

FIGURE 12.5   A sixth-grade student draws her recent experience with writing.

- **Set a "More Goal."** Gina Dignon shared this strategy, adapted from Jen Serravallo's (2015) book *The Writing Strategies Book*:

  1. Ask students to think about how many lines they usually write in five minutes and set themselves a goal to write more than that. They can mark an X on their paper to indicate the goal line.

  2. After they mark an X, you set a timer and have them write for five minutes about whatever they want.

  3. Usually, they reach their goal or go beyond it.

  4. Then they can mark an X further down the page for the remainder of the time. If they wrote four lines in five minutes, they can set an eight-line goal for ten minutes, and so on.

"I have seen this work so many times," Gina says. "Sometimes kids just have to see the lines on the page—even if it is not great writing. Seeing that they can produce some kind of volume, and have the stamina for writing, helps them get started."

Finally, try to be tolerant with your never-writers. It's important to accept their negative feelings about writing because those emotions are very real, as we can see from the drawings in this chapter.

"There is power in a drawing of a grinning student with a lightbulb over his head while sitting down to plan an essay," Sharon Zumbrunn says. "Sadly, there is also power in a drawing of a student feeding his writing into a paper shredder, thinking to himself, 'That's better,' as his writing is chewed apart by the shredder's metal teeth" (Zumbrunn et al., 2017, p. 676).

Ouch!

It may be burden to us when we have kids in our class who don't want to write, but it's a burden for them, too. And we should remind ourselves that our student identities are not fixed and permanent. Most kids have multiple identities that shift over time. *I'm a talented actor—I'm going to be on TV.* A few months later that changes to *I'm so good at basketball—I'm going to play in the NBA.* Later: *I'm going to be a scientist and figure out how to get rid of all the plastic in the ocean.*

FIGURE 12.6   A young student draws her experience with writing, noting she can't think of anything to write.

Identity is dynamic and fluid, and that's equally true of wri-dentity. In September students may feel one thing about themselves as writers, but by January they may see themselves differently.

In order for never-writers to change their attitudes, we may need to change our stance toward them. When dealing with kids with a negative wri-dentity, it's important to have a sense of humor and to maintain an upbeat attitude. Veteran teacher Mike Reynolds puts it like this:

"When students come into my class and say they like writing, I smile and say, *That's why your teacher from last year put you in my class. I'm so excited to teach you.* When students come into my class and say they don't like writing, I smile and say, *That's why your teacher from last year put you with me. I'm so excited to teach you to love it just like I do.* Kids laugh when they realize I'm saying the same thing both ways."

Tracy Cole teaches sixth grade in Birmingham, Alabama. Here she shares her strategies for dealing with students with negative wri-dentity.

The biggest thing I try to do is lay out a foundation early so I don't have a lot of negativity about writing.

1. I communicate with their teacher before I even know the students. I ask her opinion about strengths and challenges. Students select a piece of writing to share with me and answer a few questions about writing, specifically what they want me to know about them as a writer. I use that information in conversation with them the first week they're in my room. So they know I'm interested even before I meet them.

2. I set up rhythms and routines, so the flow is predictable and establishes comfort. I refer to them as writers (this has a lot of power) and share how they will live a writerly life by keeping a writer's notebook, writing daily, and learning from mentors. I have an honest conversation (whole class and one-on-one) to say that even though they may have negative feelings toward writing, I'm here to help them like it, at least a little.

3. I inspire and compliment a lot. I find something they are doing in writing, whether topic or craft, and compliment them on it. They also find out very quickly that they have to try. I'm here to help, but they must take the first step. It's hard to push back when they know you are their biggest cheerleader. Building a relationship matters.

4. I start out with daily quick writes. This is really important because they can find success in writing something small. This is also where I teach them to read like a writer.

5. We celebrate and find authentic writing experiences. When I give them real reasons to write, they start to see that their writing is important and matters for bigger reasons than just a grade.

6. I write alongside them. I make sure they see my love for writing as well as my challenges with writing.

7. I try to design opportunities for writing that are new and creative, not the same thing they have written since first grade.

8. I encourage them to write about things that are important to them.

9. They quickly learn that they can't hide in class. I'm going to be right beside them. I'm accountable to them and they are accountable to me.

10. We take time to reflect frequently about individual projects and growth in themselves.

Freewrite & Reflection

- Who are the "never-writers" in my class? Jot down one or two names.

- What attitude do I communicate to them? How might I respond to them differently?

- Which of the strategies mentioned in this chapter might help them become more receptive to writing?

Let Them Mess Around and Play

13

In all writing $E = PQ^2$. All energy in a piece of writing is equal to the play quotient of the writer squared. If a writer has no sense of play, the prose will be lifeless and anemic, as though anybody could have written it.

—Barry Lane

One rainy Saturday morning I found myself in a goofy mood. A friend had recently sent me a copy of *The Book of Ralph* by John McNally. Mailing *The Book of Ralph* to Ralph Fletcher was his idea of a sly joke, I guess, but it got me thinking. I have always had complicated feelings about my first name, especially during college when I was shocked to discover that "to ralph" is a slang way of saying "to vomit." Ugh. But now an idea sprouted in my mind. How about a fanciful story titled "Planet Ralph"?

As I said, I was in a goofy mood, so I said what the heck and gave myself permission to play around with the idea. Figure 13.1 shows a page from my notebook.

FIGURE 13.1   Planet Ralph! A page from my notebook

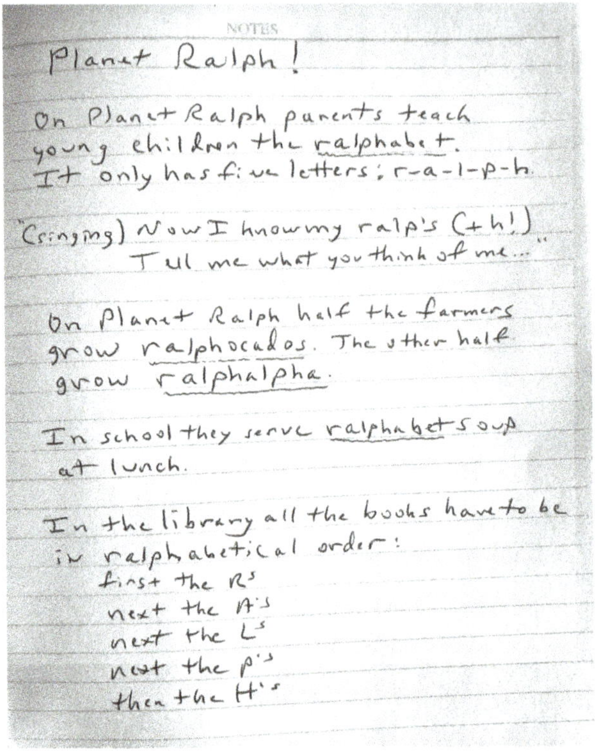

> Planet Ralph!
>
> On Planet Ralph parents teach
> young children the ralphabet.
> It only has five letters: r-a-l-p-h.
>
> (singing) Now I know my ralp's (+h!)
>   Tell me what you think of me..."
>
> On Planet Ralph half the farmers
> grow ralphocados. The other half
> grow ralphalpha.
>
> In school they serve ralphabet soup
> at lunch.
>
> In the library all the books have to be
> in ralphabetical order:
>   first the R's
>   next the A's
>   next the L's
>   next the p's
>   then the H's

Is this a great idea for a book? Who knows? Does "Planet Ralph" have any chance of getting published? I'm not holding my breath, but it has been fun riding this improbable idea, seeing how far I can take it. Experience has taught me that when I'm "writing loose," that is, playing with an idea and not being so dogged and literal, good things often happen.

This chapter is about encouraging young writers to be playful. Writing is inherently playful, and when we discourage young writers from playing with language, we rob them of an essential ingredient they need to make their lift from the tarmac and get airborne.

"The diner only gets to see the finished product," says Mike Reynolds, a literacy coach in Pennsylvania. "They don't see the mess the chef made in the kitchen to produce that meal. I think that's the way to approach teaching writing. You have to be willing to let your students experiment and be messy in order to eventually achieve that cohesive piece at the end."

Given the current state of education (the fixation on test scores and academic writing), this may seem like the wrong time to be talking about play in writing . . . which lets me know it's exactly the right time. Here are some ways to encourage play in writing. I suggest you offer them to your students as invitations, not assignments.

- **Rethink revision.** Many students perceive revision as a way to fix a broken piece. In fact, revision is an opportunity to play. Case in point: I wanted to write a poem about the Venus flytrap. My first draft was straightforward and factual. But when I reread it, I could tell that something was missing. I wondered, *What if I try writing it from the point of view of the Venus flytrap itself?* I tried that and got a livelier draft, though I still wasn't completely satisfied. Then I thought, *How about trying the poem as a rap?* When I did that, the poem snapped into place.

    Venus Fly
    yeah that's my name
    munching houseflies
    that's my game

    I like moisture
    and full sunlight
    distilled water
    tastes all right . . .

"Revising is about re-seeing, rethinking, reviewing, and transforming drafted writing," Young and Ferguson (2021b) point out in *Writing for Pleasure*. "It should be considered as a form of play. Revision stands out from all the other processes because it offers writers the chance to be at their most creative and dynamic" (p. 131).

> Revision stands out from all the other processes because it offers writers the chance to be at their most creative and dynamic.
> —Ross Young and Felicity Ferguson

Many kids have a limited perception of revision. They see it as first aid (making minor changes) as opposed to major surgery. They look at revision as a way to fix a broken piece of writing. We should remind them that revision means *to see again*. Rereading and re-visioning their drafts gives them the opportunity to be expansive and playful. They can consider the following:

- What would happen if I shift the point of view from the first person (I) to the second person (you)?
- What would happen if I started my story with sound effects?
- What would happen if I marked my strongest line and began with that?

- **Wordplay.** We fall into a trap when we think of writing as either right or wrong. Strong writers know that sometimes it's necessary to create their own rules, their own words. While I was texting with my sister, explaining why I didn't want to have dinner with a certain relative, she texted back, "Believe me, Ralph, I OVERstand!"

"Ha!" I replied. "Never heard that one before."

"That's because I just made it up," she said.

My grandson Aaron (second grade) and I were writing a story about a boy with a dog. In the story the dog had a suspicious character and wasn't entirely trustworthy.

"What kind of dog should it be?" I asked. "What breed?"

Aaron paused for a long moment before replying, "A golden re-stealer!" (Clever!)

There are many kinds of wordplay available to a writer, including puns, alliteration, onomatopoeia, hyperbole, and metaphor. I recently became aware of *sniglets,* which are words that don't actually exist, but should:

- Spudrubble—the remnants of french fries at the bottom of the container
- Flopcorn—un-popped corn kernels
- Snough—when you sneeze and cough at the same time

- **Alternative forms of writing.** In her book *Writing, Redefined,* Shawna Coppola (2019) makes a compelling case that our understanding of writing is much too narrow. She encourages teachers to broaden our definition to include nontraditional forms: visual composition (comics, video, wordless picture books, graphic writing), aural composition (podcasts, spoken word poetry), multimodal composition (infographics, memes, zines). Shawna shows that these non-alphabetical forms often favor visual learners, kids whose culture has an aural tradition, as well as struggling writers.

- **Parody.** Parody is defined as the imitation of the style of a person or genre with deliberate exaggeration for comic effect. A good example can be found at the end of Chapter 11, where two eighth-grade girls created a eulogy for the word *totally*. Usually we eulogize a person who has died, so it's fun to imagine eulogizing a word. Kids love to take a familiar form and twist it (this is particularly true of boys), so parody gives students a great chance to be playful and humorous in their writing.

- **Personal language.** Literacy coach Ana Patton envisions a writing classroom where kids might think like this: "We can write like we tell stories during lunch—using words like *bru* or *sus* and laughing when we see the expression of confusion on our teacher's face. We can stumble over words, tell jokes in fragments, say things so fast we lose our breath, and even speak words we wish we could take back. We can be messy, invent secret codes, sounds, and weird phrases . . ."

  Let's allow kids to bring bits of their own language into their writing, for example, the way Pam Muñoz Ryan (2000) does in her novel *Esperanza Rising*.

- **Break the rules.** Max, a sixth grader, wrote a piece that begins like this:

  > Did you ever crave more chocolate than you can handle? Well, I did once at my twin little brothers' 6th birthday party, and it wasn't pretty. The culprit? A compelling chocolate fountain that my mom's friend had loaned us. The victim? Me.

  If you're an English teacher, the sentence fragments (The culprit? The victim?) jump out at you. But I'd argue that these "errors" actually make the paragraph stronger by strengthening the voice, and also by offering a contrast with the longer sentences. I agree with traditionalists who insist that students should know the rules of language. But I say let them do what all writers do and break the rules from time to time, if it suits their purpose.

I know a sixth-grade boy who included a sentence fragment in the New York State writing test assessment. He circled the fragment and drew an arrow to the margin where he wrote, "Dear Corrector, I know this is a sentence fragment. I just wanted you to know that I'm using it on purpose. So please don't mark it wrong."

It's like watching one of your kids learn how to ski. When you watch your daughter skiing without falling you say to yourself, *Hey, she's skiing. She's doing it.* But when you observe her zipping off the trail into the edge of the woods to perform jumps and "get some air," you say to yourself, *Wow, she's **owning** it!*

Greenbelt Writing

A greenbelt is an invisible line designating a border around a certain area, preventing development of the area and allowing wildlife to return.

In *Joy Write: Cultivating High-Impact, Low-Stakes Writing*, I borrow the concept of a greenbelt and show how it can be brought into a writing classroom (Fletcher, 2017). The way I imagine it, kids could be invited to work on their greenbelt writing projects in parallel with the writing units the class is undertaking.

Greenbelt writing gives students total freedom to write whatever they want, without restriction—it's informal, unmanicured, and uncurated. They can write raps, plays, songs, commercials, comics, horror, science fiction . . . Barry Lane described greenbelt writing as "the writing kids love to do when nobody is looking over their shoulders."

Greenbelt writing gives kids a generous invitation to play with language. Though we never called it that, my grandson Aaron and I engaged in greenbelt writing when we collaborated on a book titled *The Sausage Club*. For the most part it was Aaron's creation, though I did contribute an idea here and there. Chapter 1 is titled "A Close Cut." Chapter 2 is "Out of the Frying Pan Into the Fire." It was great fun—when we finished I felt as proud as if I'd won the Newbery.

Later, Aaron got ambitious and began scheming about an entire book series he and I could create together. Here are some of the titles Aaron came up with:

The Worm of Destiny

The Pig of Life

The Cat of Death

The Mouse of Music

The Monkey of Madness

The Dog of Doubt

The Elephant of Embarrassment

We only got as far as the titles and never actually wrote any of these books, but I know they would be fun to write.

For one student, Henry, greenbelt writing helped unlock his creativity. When Henry was in fourth and fifth grades, he and his friends created a comic series titled "Two Idiots Who Changed the World." The boys worked on this series during an afterschool program. They even created merchandise to go along with the series—custom T-shirts that they wore at school every chance they got (Figures 13.2 and 13.3). This is a fine example of greenbelt writing: choice-driven, self-initiated, collaborative.

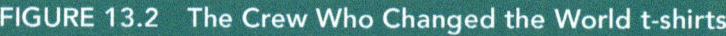

FIGURE 13.2   The Crew Who Changed the World t-shirts

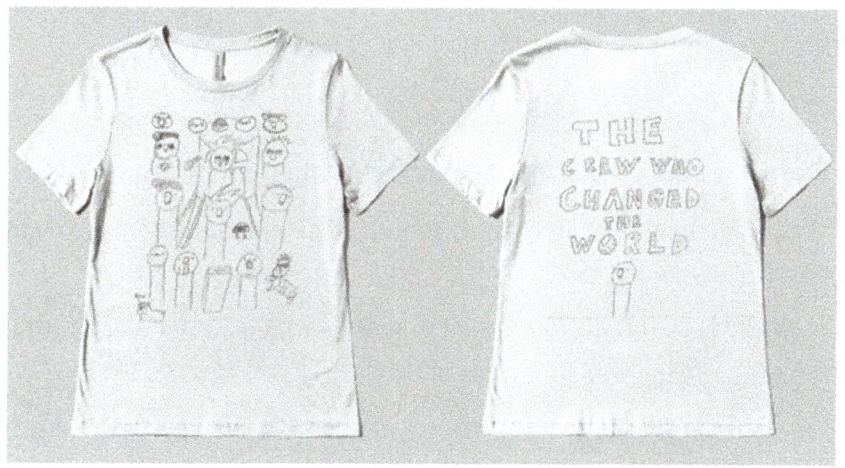

"Henry loved sharing the series with his friends," remembers Olivia Wahl, Henry's mother and creator of the *Schoolutions* podcast. "It was a HUGE privilege that Henry was the holder of the red folder that contained all the comics every day."

FIGURE 13.3   The cover to the "Two Idiots Who Changed the World" comic

Five years later, I asked Henry to reflect on this writing project.

"I loved making stuff up with my friends," Henry told me. "We thought it was really funny, too."

I asked, "How did making 'Two Idiots Who Changed the World' differ from the writing you did in school?"

"It wasn't assigned so I felt like I had more freedom to write what I wanted," Henry says. "There wasn't a rubric or anything so I didn't feel like anything was right or wrong. It was just for fun."

In her book *Enchantment: Awakening Wonder in an Anxious World*, Katherine May (2023) reminds us that play is strongly linked with identity: "Play is the complete absorption in something that doesn't matter to the external world, but which matters completely to you. It's an immersion in your own interests that becomes a feeling in itself, a potent emotion. Play is a disappearance into a space of our choosing, invisible to those outside the game. It is the pursuit of pure flow, a sandbox mind in which we can test new thoughts, new selves" (p. 136).

When young writers are playing they're focused, in the zone, totally engaged. They're motivated to write. I know I am. As soon as I finish this chapter I'm going back to my Planet Ralph project. I'm thinking the story will take place in an imaginary country where the official national food is ralphioli . . .

Freewrite & Reflection

- When has being playful helped me learn something?

- What might be the value in encouraging students to be playful in their writing?

- How can I show students that I value "greenbelt writing"?

Invite Reflection

> I feel most like a writer when I'm alone and quiet . . . when all the noise and thoughts are in my head waiting to be put on paper.
>
> —Emi, fifth-grade student

Reflection was all the rage when my sons were in school. The prevailing term was *metacognition*: thinking about thinking. The rationale was that becoming aware of your thinking will improve the way you learn. It's a compelling idea, and one that quickly made its way into the classroom. When my sons were in middle school, their LA teachers frequently asked, "What did you learn about yourself as a reader after reading this book?" Or, "What did you learn about yourself as a writer after writing this piece?"

My sons were impatient with questions like that. They wanted to read, they wanted to write, but they wanted no part of this additional metacognitive loop. It struck them as busy work. And it didn't resonate with who they were as learners, at least not at that point in their lives.

"'What did I learn about myself as a reader?'" Taylor fumed when he was in middle school. "What does that even mean? I finished the book, and I loved it! I love *The Wheel of Time* series! That's what I learned—but I already knew that!"

Like any parent, I was influenced by my kids' reaction, perhaps overly so. I wondered why our kids balked at reflecting on themselves as learners. Several teachers told me anecdotally that metacognition seems to come more naturally to the girls in class. Could my son's gender be a significant factor?

For these reasons I became wary of reflection. I could see the potential value, though I suspected we were overdoing the whole metacognition thing. But in recent years my thinking on this issue has evolved. I have seen that students build wri-dentity when given the opportunity to reflect on themselves as writers.

When and How to Invite Reflection

I recommend inviting reflection at the beginning of the school year and also closer to the end. Ask your students to complete this sentence:

I'm the kind of writer who. . . .

See Figures 14.1 and 14.2 for two students' responses to that prompt. You can also ask your students to answer these questions:

- Are you a writer?

- When do you feel most like a writer?

- What activities or assignments make you feel most like a writer?

Hopefully you'll discover that students have deepened their wri-dentity during their time in your classroom. Strategies for inviting reflection, with powerful student response examples, follow next in this chapter.

FIGURE 14.1   One student, Emersyn, reflects on his writing identity

FIGURE 14.2 Another student reflects on their writing identity

I'm the kind of writer who needs to be able to write fiction.

Invite Students to Reflect on Their Wri-dentity

Sara Tillett asked her students, "Are you a writer?" One ninth grader, Bella, responded like this:

> I think I am a writer. I do not define a "writer" as someone who writes professionally for a living or someone with great techniques. I think a writer is someone who treats each piece of writing seriously, invests effort into their work, and always tries to perfect their writing. Famous writers are successful not because they learned how to write, but because they care about their writing and are devoted to it. In this definition, I am a writer.

"When do you feel most like a writer?" Sara asked her students. Seventh grader Natalia responded,

> I feel most like a writer when I'm fully engaged in my writing. If it is a school project or just for fun, I feel most like a writer when the noises around me are blurred and I'm in the story and not just the writer. I also feel like a writer when I hit a wall but push through anyways. There is something amazing about rewriting a sentence till it clicks. That moment where your perseverance pays off is when I feel most like a writer.

AJ, a boy in Ann Marie Corgill's fifth-grade class in Alabama, answered the questions like this:

I feer like a writer

When I am sharing
my story to the class,
When I'm getting ideas,
and when I free write.

AJ

Reflection like this will solidify a student's wri-dentity. Often students are being asked to think about something they have never considered before! Reflecting gives them a chance to excavate this tacit knowledge and claim it. It's a chance for the student to think aloud and explain what kind of writer he or she is.

Ask Students to Reflect on Their Writing Journey

Penny Kittle invited her first-year college students to give a video "Notebook Tour" in which they could talk about their writer's notebook. In her video, student Jorja shared her realizations about how she had changed as a writer during the school year:

> Look how little there is on this page. [Jorja turns the page.]
> Okay, so it got a little better here. [She turns the page again.]
> Oh, my God! I wrote so much! I didn't have, like, more time
> to do it. I just, like, grew! Like, I learned! My skills had grown.
> I accomplished a lot more. And it's really cool to look back
> and see your growth. And this has only been, like, what? Over
> a three-month period? Imagine what I could do over a whole
> year. Or two years!

It's an opportunity for students to tell the story of themselves as writers, to reflect on how they've changed and grown over the course of the year.

https://qrs.ly/ ingwtpc

Scan the QR code to watch Jorja's video.

Invite Students to Reflect on When They Feel Like a Writer

Many of our students have writing lives that will remain hidden and invisible until we give them a chance to talk about them. An eighth-grade student was asked when do they feel like a writer:

> A hobby of mine is drawing frogs. I draw frogs to hang on my bedroom wall. All different kinds and such, and right next to the picture I drew of the frog I write a description of the frog maybe a paragraph and a half, nothing too crazy. I definitely feel like a writer then.

Another eighth grader responded,

> I feel most like a writer when I am writing poems but in my case, songs. I write songs all the time on my guitar and piano. I have written over 150 songs and am actually working on some big projects that revolve around that right now.

See Figure 14.3 for another sample response.

One eighth grader had this reply to the question *What activities have helped you feel most like a writer?*

> Anything with writing that I choicefully participate in: clubs, writing contests, free writing, etc. assist with the feeling of being a writer. School-related assignments that involve topics I'm interested in writing about (certain parts of history, current issues, argumentative topics, and other assignments that have many personal choices involved in them) help me feel like a writer. Activities that entail writing on the more creative side, poetry and stories rather than essays, give me the feeling of being a true writer, and not just someone who is being required to write.

> FIGURE 14.3   Reflection from a fifth-grade student

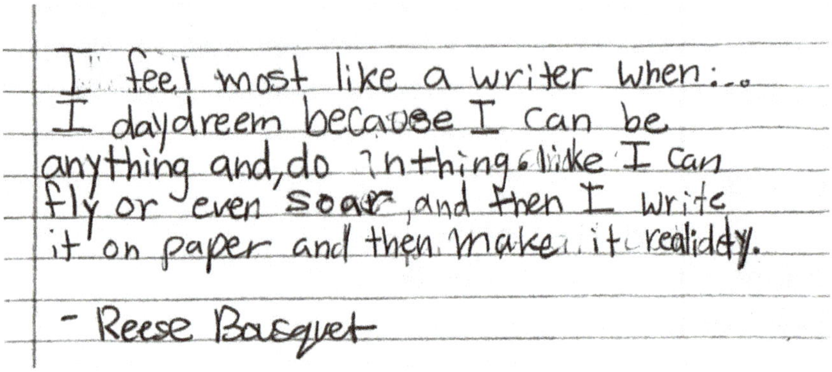

I feel most like a writer when...
I daydreem becaose I can be
anything and do anithing like I can
fly or even soar, and then I write
it on paper and then make it realiddy.

— Reese Basquet

Encourage Reflection That's Honest

Reflection provides us with important data, but it's not always good news. When students are encouraged to reply honestly, some will admit that they don't perceive themselves as writers.

Are you a writer? "Not outside of ELA class," one fifth-grade boy wrote. "I feel like I only enjoy writing when I'm not being forced to do it. Also, I want to be able to choose and not be forced to write about my opinion on something random."

That's another benefit to these reflections—they help us examine our teaching. We can see which activities help kids connect to writing and which do not. We may be dismayed to learn that certain activities actually work against building wri-dentity.

Ask Students to Reflect on an Individual Piece of Writing

So far we've been talking about self-reflection. But you might also ask students to reflect on an individual piece of writing. At the end of the year, Kelly Gallagher asked students to select one piece of writing and answer the following questions:

- If you had a little more time to work on this, what would you have done?

- What was difficult about this paper?

"Having them spend ten minutes on a half-page reflect is worth the time investment," Kelly says.

Support Reflection With Volume and Choice

As I said at the beginning of this chapter, I've revised my thinking on reflection. There's definitely value in inviting students to describe their emerging writer selves. But Penny Kittle offers a cautionary note, reminding us that true reflection must be supported by volume and choice.

"In many classrooms students aren't writing enough to make that reflection real and valuable," Penny says. "If a student writes four things in a semester, and each one is detailed in its form and attached to a rubric, the student will be reflecting what the teacher said, not their own thinking and analysis of their growth."

Passion and investment are crucial to a young writer. Kids aren't going to grow as writers if they're just going through the motions, doing test prep, or following a writing script. If it's boring they'll check out—or act out. The research of Mary Helen Immordino-Yang (2016), an educational psychologist at the University of Southern California, demonstrates that emotion is crucial to learning. Students have to care about what they're writing. Ruby, a ninth-grade student, explained it this way:

> The smallest things in a regular moment can spark creativity
> at the most unexpected times. These ideas can come from
> something as simple as the sound of the snow crunching
> or noticing a familiar bird call. For me this is what makes
> writing so special. When you find the perfect way to embody
> the feeling of a moment into your writing, it instantly
> becomes powerful and relatable. Feeling the words coming
> to you and knowing that it is describing exactly how you feel
> is unmatchable. It is empowering to know that you have your
> own ideas stored and can use them when you can't find a way
> to convey the idea in the moment. I feel most like a writer
> when this happens because I am thinking about writing
> instinctively.

CHAPTER 14

Never knew that could write good.

The What and the How

Dan Feigelson has been a classroom teacher (PS 321 in Brooklyn), a researcher, a principal (PS 6 in Manhattan), and a superintendent. He has published several books, including *Reading Projects Reimagined: Student-Driven Conferences to Deepen Critical Thinking* (2014). This is an excerpt from an informal interview I did when he and I discussed the notion of wri-dentity.

A big percentage of identity, in almost anything, is the WHAT and the HOW. Most people can tell you WHAT they like to read—mysteries, romance, nonfiction, etc. But often they don't have a sense of HOW they read. *Am I someone who tends to visualize? Am I someone who asks a lot of questions? Am I someone who stops in places and thinks back on earlier parts of the book?* These are different ways people make meaning in their head. When someone points that out to students, they sit up straight and say to themselves, *Yeah, I can do that. That is the kind of reader I am.* It bolsters their sense of identity.

This applies to writing. WHAT do you do? Do you write long florid emails . . . . or do you get very terse in your emails? Do you write journal entries? Are you someone who scribbles poetry on the back of your notebook?

On top of that there's the HOW—the things you do as a writer. For me, for example, when I write I'm always conscious of using a variety of sentence lengths and sentence types. Periodically when I write I stop and look back and think, *Wow, three long sentences in a row. Not good.* So I'll revise. I'll break up long sentences and put in shorter ones. Or, I see I've had too many simple declarative sentences, so I'll put in a more complex one. I'm very conscious of that because in my head I'm always thinking of the rhythm, the sound, the melody, the music of the language.

Most kids don't typically reflect on the HOW. What goes alongside that is connecting the HOW to the desired outcome. If I want my reader to visualize, a really good thing to do is to describe a physical action.

That's true with almost anything. If I'm a baseball player, part of my identity is I can see where the holes are in the outfield and hit the ball to those holes. There are things you know to do. You have a tool chest. And feeling like you have a tool chest that you can consciously use is part of having a sense of identity around anything.

It comes back to WHAT and the HOW. One way to promote identity in writing is to catch them in the act of doing certain things—*Wow, Olivia, I notice something you do in your writing is when you write dialogue, you combine dialogue with action. That's something I notice in a lot of your writing. And it really helps me create a movie in my mind.* And Olivia thinks, *Yeah! Part of my wri-dentity is I can combine dialogue with description.* As a teacher, I name that, I shine a light on that. Maybe Olivia has never thought of that before. And as a teacher, I could maybe push her a little further: *You could do dialogue and external description combined with varying the signifiers: using* exclaimed *or* shouted *instead of* said.

Freewrite & Reflection

- What steps could I take to encourage students to reflect on themselves as writers?

- How might modeling this (reflecting on my own growth as a writer) encourage my students to do so?

Lingering Thoughts About Building Wri-dentity

15

My goal in writing this book is simple but ambitious:

> I want all our students to see themselves as writers.

Writing is a peculiar thing. In 1993 I published a book titled *What A Writer Needs*. In 2008 I created a video titled *Dude, Listen to This! Engaging Boy Writers*. At one point I looked into the camera and declared, "Everything we do should be geared toward creating life-long writers."

I can see now that I have been thinking about wri-dentity for a long time, though I didn't realize it at the time.

Cultural identity is multi-layered, deep, and steadfast. But if you spend time around children you know that day-to-day identity is fluid and fearless. *I'm going to be an astronaut. I'm going to be president.* When my son Robert was seven I asked him what he wanted to be when he grew up.

"A football player and a writer," he told me.

I smiled to myself, thinking that a person couldn't do both, that you had to choose one identity or another. But who's to say? In fact, some football players do end up writing books (Dan Jenkins' *Semi-Tough*, for instance). Professional athletes often retire in their early thirties, leaving them plenty of time to write.

Claiming identity in writing or anything else isn't something that happens overnight. It takes time.

Case in point: My wife and I recently decided to keep bees. We purchased two hives, and JoAnn painted them to protect the wood against harsh New Hampshire winters. We also bought the necessary paraphernalia: a smoker to calm the bees, feeder, plus the bee outfit (jacket, gloves, and a veil to protect the neck and head when you have to inspect the hive). There are bears in our town, so we also purchased a solar-powered bear fence. Ka-ching!

We have ordered two "nucs" (the word is short for nucleus): a colony of live bees that comes with eggs, brood, and a few thousand bees (including a queen). In a few days we'll go pick them up, drive them home, and start the hive.

There's a ton to learn about beekeeping, and we're trying to educate ourselves. We have watched YouTube videos, read *Beekeeping for Dummies* (highly recommended), and joined the Seacoast Beekeepers Association, a local group of fellow beekeepers. We have three mentors, guys with years of experience who have given us invaluable information and answered dozens of questions. Jeff, the one who sold us the hives, manages 200+ hives of his own!

Soon I'll have photos of myself, in full regalia, inspecting one of the frames from our hive while bees froth all around me, like bubbles around a scuba diver. At that point will I describe myself a beekeeper? Will I have claimed my "bee-dentity?"

No.

Even after we bring the two bee colonies home, even after both hives are humming and (hopefully) filling with honey, I won't be able to say that. Not yet. There's a world of difference, a million miles between saying *I'm keeping bees* to declaring *I'm a beekeeper*. I'll get there eventually, but it will take time, a lot more learning, getting stung once or twice, maybe a disaster or two, before I can confidently claim that identity.

Each chapter in this book offers an approach that will help students build their identity as writers. I've come to the end of the book, but not the end of the conversation because it's my most fervent hope that this book sparks dialogue. I still have ongoing conversations in my head, questions I didn't address in this book, one of which I hope you'll reflect on in your own classroom:

> Could we make the writing classroom more kinetic and less static? Translated: Could we create classrooms where kids could be kids and move around when they feel the need to do so? I suspect that one change might help kids feel more at home in the writing classroom, and help them see themselves as writers.

I want to leave you with a few other ideas to consider as you foster your students' wri-dentity:

- **Center talk in claiming wri-dentity.** "The more kids talk about their process—how they did something—the more they make strategies available to others," says Peter Johnston, author of *Choice Words* (2004). "Also, as they articulate strategies they used, the more they are able to transfer those strategies to other contexts. The more they attend to the process, the more they are likely to adopt a growth mindset which has a lot of benefits."

- **Celebrate the rich "funds of knowledge" every kid brings to school.**

- **Normalize frustration and failure in writing.**

- **Challenge young writers.** It's important to affirm and support them, but it's also okay to nudge them when you sense they're coasting.

- **Offer occasional prompts and quick-writes.** I believe in helping students find and write about issues they know and care about. But there's also a place for giving kids a prompt every so often, an opportunity for them to ride the energy and eloquence of a strong text, to emulate its substance or style. Often students are shocked at what they can create in a short burst of writing.

Riding the Wave

I got to witness something special one summer day on a Cape Cod beach. We were hanging out, enjoying the late afternoon sun, when two fathers showed up with their young daughters, all four of them wearing wet suits. The dads and daughters were going surfing. The girls were quite young. The conditions at the shore couldn't have been more perfect: low tide, no wind, tame waves that were still big enough to ride. The dads carried the girls' surfboards through the soft sand and handed them to the girls at the water's edge.

Suddenly there was a commotion. One of the girls had a meltdown and started to cry. From that distance I couldn't see what was wrong . . . maybe her wetsuit didn't feel right? I wondered if the outing would fall apart before it began. But her father didn't get flustered. He knelt down, listened quietly to his daughter, and managed to soothe her feelings.

A few minutes later the foursome waded into the shallow water and began swimming away from the shore. The dads showed the girls how to grasp their boards and bob over the waves. Finally they reached the right place. A wave arrived and one of the girls wanted to take it. But the father didn't launch her. He eased her forward, coaching her with words I couldn't hear. The girl paddled hard and caught the wave. She jumped up onto her surfboard!

She was up! Standing! We all wanted to clap. We DID clap! The ride only lasted a few seconds before the girl leaned to one side and toppled over. Moments later she popped up to the surface, wiping wet hair from her face.

"I wiped out!" she called to her dad. She looked despondent, but her father had a wide grin.

"You did great!" he called back. "C'mon, let me see you do another!"

The surfing lessons continued. Sometimes the girls surfed side by side, and you could see the difference in their styles. One girl crouched down low on her board; the other seemed more playful, riding with her tongue out.

It was a clinic for teaching any difficult skill. What a rich learning environment! So many important conditions were present:

- **Mentors.** The two men were both experienced surfers.

- **Immersion.** The focus was on doing, not talking. The two men knew the girls would learn to surf by surfing lots of waves.

- **Strong relationships.** Their fathers gave them love, patience, and time.

- **Social**. They were all doing it together.

- **Vibe**. It felt loose, casual, and fun.

- **Failure.** The dads expected the girls to wipe out, so they celebrated it when it happened.

- **Zone of proximal development**. The dads gave their kids a challenge that was real but manageable, the waves not too big and not too small.

- **Externals**. Wetsuits and surfboards.

Talk about claiming identity! Who could doubt that those girls would eventually come to see themselves as surfers?

That's what I want for our writers. I want to create classrooms where they can wade into the ocean every day, wait for a "wave" that speaks to them, and jump on. I don't care if they wipe out—I'm sure they will—but I want them to experience for themselves the unique thrill of riding a writing wave, hearing it hiss and murmur, feeling the power as it surges forward, and seeing just how far it can take them.

References

Ahmed, S. (2018). *Being the change: Lessons and strategies to teach social comprehension.* Heinemann.

Anderson, C. (2024). *Teaching fantasy writing.* Corwin.

Anderson, C., & Glover, M. (2023). *Becoming a better writing teacher.* Heinemann.

Anderson, M. D. (2020). *Becoming a teacher.* Simon & Schuster.

Atwell, N. (1998). *In the middle: New understandings about writing, reading, and learning.* Heinemann.

Bloom, B. (1985). *Developing talent in young people.* Random House.

Bomer, K. (2010). *Hidden gems: Naming and teaching from the brilliance in every student's writing.* Heinemann.

Brooks, D. (2025, March 27). A surprising route to the best life possible. *New York Times.* https://www.nytimes.com/2025/03/27/opinion/persistence-work-difficulty.html

Coppola, S. (2019). *Writing, redefined: Broadening our ideas of what it means to compose.* Routledge.

Cremin, T., Myhill, D., Eyres, I., & Nash, T. (2019, September). Teachers as writers: Learning together with others. *Literacy, 54*(4). http://doi.org/10.1111/lit.12201

Davies, N. (2004). *Bat loves the night.* Candlewick Press.

Denton, P. (2013). *The power of our words* (2nd ed.). Center for Responsive Schools.

Dorfman, L., & Cappelli, R. (2007). *Mentor texts: Teaching writing through children's literature, K–6.* Routledge.

Elbow, P. (1998). *Writing with power.* Oxford University Press.

Feigelson, D. (2014). *Reading projects reimagined: Student-driven conferences to deepen critical thinking.* Heinemann.

Fletcher, R. (1993). *What a writer needs.* Heinemann.

Fletcher, R. (1996). *A writer's notebook: Unlocking the writer within you.* HarperCollins.

Fletcher, R. (1999). *Relatively speaking: Poems about family.* Scholastic.

Fletcher, R. (2006). *Boy writers: Reclaiming their voices.* Routledge.

Fletcher, R. (2008). *Dude, listen to this! Engaging boy writers* [Video]. Stenhouse.

Fletcher, R. (2011). *Mentor author, mentor texts.* Heinemann.

Fletcher, R. (2017). *Joy write: Cultivating high-impact, low-stakes writing.* Heinemann.

Fox, M. (1993). *Radical reflections.* HarperCollins.

Gallagher, K., & Kittle, P. (2018). *180 days: Two teachers and the quest to engage and empower adolescents.* Heinemann.

Gardner, P. (2014). Becoming a teacher of writing: Primary student teachers reviewing their relationship with writing. *English in Education, 48*(2), 128–148.

Gladwell, M. (2008). *Outliers: The story of success.* Little, Brown.

Glover, M. (2019). *Craft and process studies: Units that provide writers with choice of genre.* Heinemann.

Glover, M., & Keene, E. (Eds.). (2015). *The teacher you want to be: Essays about children, learning, and teaching.* Heinemann.

Gonzalez, J. (2020, October 12). Subversion: An essential tool of the master teacher. *The

Cult of Pedagogy. https://www.cultofpedagogy.com/subversion/

Graves, D. H. (1983). *Writing: Teachers and children at work.* Heinemann.

Greene, M. (1988). *The dialectic of freedom.* Teachers College Press.

Grimes, N. (2019). *Ordinary hazards: A memoir.* Wordsong.

Harvey, S., & Ward, A. (2017). *From striving to thriving: How to grow confident, capable readers.* Scholastic.

Immordino-Yang, M. H. (2016). *Ed-Talk: Learning with an emotional brain* [Video]. YouTube. https://www.youtube.com/watch?v=DEe0350WQrsJohnston, P. (2004). *Choice words: How our language affects children's learning.* Stenhouse.

Keene, E. (2018). *Engaging children: Igniting a drive for deeper learning.* Heinemann.

King Farris, Christine. (2006). *My brother Martin: A sister remembers growing up with the Rev. Dr. Martin Luther King Jr.* Scholastic.

Laman, T. (2013). *From ideas to words: Writing strategies for English language learners.* Heinemann.

Lyons, G. E. (n.d.). *Where I'm from.* George Ella Lyons. http://www.georgeellalyon.com/where.html

Marshak, S. (1991). *I am the ocean.* Arcade.

May, K. (2023). *Enchantment: Awakening wonder in an anxious world.* Riverhead Books.

Meehan, M. (2022). *Answers to your biggest questions about teaching elementary writing.* Corwin.

Miller, D., & Callahan, E. (2022). *I'm the kind of kid who...: Invitations that support learning identity and agency.* Heinemann.

Muñoz Ryan, P. (2000). *Esperanza rising.* Scholastic.

National Council of Teachers of English. (2022, August 29). *Position statement on writing instruction in school.* https://ncte.org/statement/statement-on-writing-instruction-in-school/

National Literacy Trust. (2024). *Children and young people's writing in 2024.* https://literacytrust.org.uk/research-services/research-themes/writing/

Newkirk, T. (2023). *Literacy's democratic roots: A personal tour through 8 big ideas.* Heinemann.

Qarooni, N. (2023). *Nourishing caregiver collaborations: Elevating home experiences and classroom practices for collective care.* Routledge.

Ray, K. W., & Villalba, S. (2025). *Wondrous words: Reimagining writers and writing in the elementary classroom.* NCTE.

Santman, D. (2005). *Shades of meaning: Comprehension and interpretation in middle school.* Heinemann.

Serravallo, J. (2015). *The reading strategies book: Your everything guide to developing skilled readers.* Heinemann.

Shubitz, S., & Dorfman, L. (2019). *Welcome to writing workshop: Engaging today's students with a model that works.* Pembroke.

Smith, M. & Wilhelm, J. (2002). *Reading don't fix no Chevys: Literacy in the lives of young men.* Pearson Education.

Srinivasan, D. (2021). *What I am.* Viking.

Stern, P. (Director). (2006). *Raising Cain: Exploring the inner lives of America's boys.* PBS Video.

Wilson, M. (2017). *Reimagining writing assessment: From scales to stories.* Heinemann.

Young, R. (2019). *What is it writing for pleasure teachers do that makes the difference?* The Goldsmiths' Company & The University of Sussex. https://writing4pleasure.com/wp-content/uploads/2019/09/what-is-it-writing-for-pleasure-teachers-do-that-makes-the-difference-report.pdf

Young, R., & Ferguson, F. (2021a). *Real-world writers: A handbook for teaching writing with 7–11 year olds.* Routledge.

Young, R., & Ferguson, F. (2021b). *Writing for pleasure: Research, theory and practice.* Routledge.

Zumbrunn, S., Ekholm, E., Stringer, J. K., McKnight, K., & DeBusk-Lane, M. (2017). Student experiences with writing: Taking the temperature of the classroom. *The Reading Teacher, 70*(6), 667–677.

Zumbrunn, S., & Krause, K. (2012). Conversations with leaders: Principles of effective writing instruction. *The Reading Teacher, 65*(5), 346–353.

Index

Because All Teachers Are Leaders

Maria Walther

Discover 50 *more* read-aloud experiences designed to bolster students' literacy development, ignite imagination, and enhance motivation.

Kayla Briseño, Gretchen Bernabei

Over 40 low-prep, high-impact lessons that explore the unexpected wonder of nonfiction picture books.

Carl Anderson

Learn how to include a study of fantasy writing in your writing curriculum that will engage student interest and creativity—and make writing exciting for them again.

Wiley Blevins

Implement effective phonics instruction with these powerful routines that help teachers differentiate whole-class lessons, so students at every skill level can engage.

Jennifer Serravallo

Nine effective, predictable, research-based lesson structures that help busy teachers save planning time and focus their teaching—and student attention—on content rather than procedures.

Sonja Cherry-Paul

Foster identity-inspiring learning experiences where students can show up completely as themselves and recognize the full humanity of all people.

At Corwin Literacy we have put together a collection of just-in-time, classroom-tested, practical resources from trusted experts that allow you to quickly find the information you need when you need it.

Brett Vogelsinger

Discover strategies to use AI thoughtfully in every stage of the writing process—without compromising creativity or critical thinking.

Jarred Amato

Create a classroom environment where independent reading thrives to help students achieve huge gains in all areas of literacy, learning, and civic engagement.

Brian Sztabnik, Susan Barber

The ultimate toolkit for teachers looking to foster motivation, creativity, and active participation that deepens learning for every student in their ELA classroom.

Rebecca G. Harper

Discover engaging lessons to transform your elementary writing instruction through a collection of 43 meticulously crafted lessons.

Douglas Fisher, Nancy Frey, Sarah Ortega, Kierstan Barbee, Aida Allen-Rotell

Recharge reading practices for adolescent readers and help educators increase foundational reading skills in the classroom.

Matthew Johnson

Practical, on-the-ground solutions for making grammar and language instruction more accessible, practical, and connected to students' reading and writing.

Free professional learning from leading education experts

 **Live and on-demand webinars**

Get a certificate for PD hours!

 **Videos**

 **Podcasts**

 **Study guides**

 **New teacher toolkit**

 **Lessons and strategies**

 **Checklists and assessments**

 **Plain language summaries of education research**

 **Book excerpts**

 **Other downloadables**

 **Blogs**

Leave a review!
If you enjoyed this book, let us know by leaving a review on **GoodReads.com** or **Amazon.com**.

corwin.com/resources

 **CORWIN**

CORWIN

To help every educator help every student

We believe that every single student deserves a great education

We believe that knowing our impact is both a privilege and a responsibility

We believe that a fair, stable, and thriving society is built on education